Desire MAKES THE DIFFERENCE

A Memoir

JASMINE CARRIETTÉ

DESIRE MAKES THE DIFFERENCE
A MEMOIR

Copyright © 2016 Jasmine Carrietté.

All rights reserved. No part of this book may be used or reproduced by any means, graphic, electronic, or mechanical, including photocopying, recording, taping or by any information storage retrieval system without the written permission of the author except in the case of brief quotations embodied in critical articles and reviews.

iUniverse books may be ordered through booksellers or by contacting:

iUniverse
1663 Liberty Drive
Bloomington, IN 47403
www.iuniverse.com
1-800-Authors (1-800-288-4677)

Because of the dynamic nature of the Internet, any web addresses or links contained in this book may have changed since publication and may no longer be valid. The views expressed in this work are solely those of the author and do not necessarily reflect the views of the publisher, and the publisher hereby disclaims any responsibility for them.

Note From the Author:

While the events in this book are true, all names and some identifying details have been changed to protect the privacy of individuals.

Any people depicted in stock imagery provided by Shutterstock are models, and such images are being used for illustrative purposes only. Certain stock imagery © Shutterstock. Cover photo credits to Art of Life.

ISBN: 978-1-4917-9861-4 (sc)
ISBN: 978-1-4917-9859-1 (hc)
ISBN: 978-1-4917-9860-7 (e)

Library of Congress Control Number: 2016908779

Print information available on the last page.

iUniverse rev. date: 05/27/2016

"I've heard said by some that the most motivating forces in their lives have been anger, dissatisfaction, defensiveness, but Jasmine Carriette's engine of pure desire fuels this book from the hot furnace of its beating heart. Hers is a story propelled by an irrepressible and unashamed appetite to be loved. She lives her life on these pages, splayed out, raw and vulnerable yet wholly without apology. I admire her grit, her language and her unbound longing, for it is finally *that* which rises up from the pages and stands out as courage, as relentlessness, as the sparkling mirror of honesty."
—Cyn Kitchen, Associate Professor of English, Knox College, and author of *Ten Tongues*.

"A spellbinding and riveting memoir, this book brings us a unique account of one woman's journey through a life of love and desire. In reading this book, other women, as well, may come to a deeper understanding of their own search for the meaning of love and sensuality and relationship in their lives." —Bonnie Strickland, PhD, Former President, American Psychological Association

FOREWORD

What do you do when you are a highly sexed female, smart and curious and driven, born in the conservative South in the 1930s? What do you do when your mother tells you that your breasts are abnormally large and you are warned away from wearing sweaters? When you are afraid that the boyfriend you adore and who adores you will cast you out after marriage and so you marry the man of your parents' dreams, a good man whose fear of sex equals your own interest in it?

You suffer and you make bad choices. You struggle, and you continue to struggle long after the end of the early marriage. You reach out for acceptance as well as for adventure. You look to find ways to bring together sex and love. You strive to understand.

And, if you are Jasmine Carrietté, you write.

Here is a memoir that is no more conventional than the life Jasmine has lived. *Desire Makes the Difference* is a memoir that will fascinate and touch you. It lets us see with sometimes brutal honesty the struggles, defeats, and victories of one woman.

But even as we learn the story of one woman, the book provides a window to all our humanity. Here we see the quest to make the spirit flesh, to let the spirit live through the flesh and in the flesh. Who among us has not dealt with the same problems and issues? And all among us will be glad to find how one very talented woman has put into words the struggles that might otherwise stay unvoiced.

This book has been a long time in the making. That I know firsthand. More than two decades ago, I was the lucky advisor to Jasmine's Smith

Scholar project. Then Jasmine graduated from Smith College where she had been part of the Ada Comstock Scholars Program, and my own career brought me to California. Jasmine and I lost touch; but I never forgot the vibrant person who asked so many questions and pushed so many boundaries. Imagine my delight in receiving an e-mail from Jasmine's editor asking me to read the manuscript and to consider writing a brief preface.

When the manuscript arrived electronically, I put aside all the pressing administrative work before, from which, to be truthful, a short break would have been welcome. I started reading. In one long sitting, with interruptions only for meals, I was swept along page after page. Jasmine's openness and honesty kept me reading long after I should have returned to my duller pursuits.

Now, with Jasmine's vivid images still before me, with the struggles of her life echoing in my consciousness, I know I will continue to ponder the interminglings of words, spirits, and flesh. What is made manifest and what remains below the surface? How do agency and surrender intermix? What is the nature of desire, erotic and otherwise? Indeed, is there such a thing as non-erotic desire?

I feel deeply honored to be asked, so many years after our work together, to pen this preface. It was a privilege to read the manuscript, some parts of which I had seen in earlier draft.

No doubt every reader will have an individual response to the pains and the joys laid out on these pages. The writing is very personal. Idiosyncratic you might say. And so, I know, will be the readers' responses. I also know that it would be hard for any reader, no matter who, to finish the book untouched.

It is clear that you know now, dear Jasmine, that you are loved. And if you will allow yourself to enter without defense into the life of Jasmine Carriette, dear reader, you will learn that you too are loved and that you too are more lovable than you may have sometimes feared.

Faye J. Crosby, PhD
Carmel, California
April, 2016

He was a man past fifty who had spent all his adult years behind the counter of a bank and by patient labour and courtesy he had risen to the position of second cashier.

—Graham Greene, *A Sense of Reality*

As a young woman I read this and thought it one of the saddest things I had ever read. I carried it in my wallet for more than twenty years, but I made a decision that day I would never live my life that way.

This book is dedicated to David Cason, a brilliant electrical engineer who now lives in Texas. But he was a student at Louisiana State University and in my Sunday school class at eighteen when I was twenty-eight. He is the first person who ever suggested I go to college. And I love him for that. Fifty-four years late, David, you have my eternal gratitude.

LOUISIANA

FEED TROUGHS

Deprivation and aloneness were all I knew of life, but somehow the isolation of rain made it all unbearable. Inevitably, on rainy days I headed for the feed trough in the barn. Its shape and size, the concealment of it, the hugging from both sides of its narrow width, coupled with the tinny sound of rain on the roof, made the panic of the passing hours controllable. So, rather than mourning, I held the time in contemplation.

Often I sat with my back against the sloping sides of the trough, my buttocks on the flat bottom, and my legs spread up the opposite slope, dangling and swinging back and forth, as I watched the rain pelting just outside the barn door. To my left, on a slightly raised wooden platform at the other side of the stable, was my mother's washer with the new automatic wringer and the two washtubs for rinsing. Just outside was an evergreen where a tree frog lived. On Saturdays, as I waited impatiently to transfer the clothes from one tub to the other for my mother, I always watched that tree frog. He fascinated me. I watched the expansion of his throat when he croaked, and the thinning of the green of his body, his delicate color. I admired his steadfastness; every week, he was always there. Farther off to the left was the garage that housed the car. It was a much older model than any of my friends' fathers' cars, but I would be unaware of that until years later. Beyond it all, the quintessential chinaberry tree. Later, I would know there was one in every Southern novel. Now, it was a major part of my life, for every night I climbed that tree to spend the evening on top of this very barn. Every night I came down off the barn about nine, but it would be fifty years before I got out of the trough.

My Mother

She had a little screwed-up mouth that she held in a peculiar way. For me, it became her trademark. Even now, as I remember her, it is in this way: her mouth twisted in a puckered grimace. She had long, slender, attractive hands, and she always spoke with her first two fingers across her mouth and her palm cupped over her chin.

That is *when* she talked. Mostly she didn't—talk that is. I'm not sure why she kept up the silence. It had long since failed to achieve any original purpose it might have had. I'm sure I'm right about this, for no one paid any attention anymore. Her silence no longer created any tension in the house. It was simply, "Tell your father dinner is ready." I probably got so verbal because I grew up speaking for two. For weeks on end she communicated with my daddy only through me or my sister, Jessica. No one thought her silence strange anymore, but I was never sure why she kept up the practice. As far as I could tell, it never got her what she wanted.

Daddy's attitude never altered one iota either way, whether she happened to be speaking that day or not. He just went about his chores as usual, nodding and pleasant. For weeks she did not speak. She pouted. If I was his wife and needed to get his attention, I'd have burned down the house or something—but, by God, I'd have gotten a reaction. I got to hate people who wouldn't talk. I find them the meanest, orneriest, most cantankerous kind of folks. They just sit there like a knot, like a bump on a log, taking up space, being angry, but venting no fury, never moving on with their lives and never resolving anything. All that energy just wasted. Some of the largest group of people who don't talk, of course, happen to be male. That'd be a problem for me later, but now, right now, I hated the example she set for me. I determined I'd never be like that, just waiting to be acted upon and never sticking up for myself. I learned to talk.

My mother had to be one of the unhappiest people I ever knew. Most of her life she was sad and bitter. I never quite figured out who or what or why she hated so much; but bitterness is the overwhelming image that comes to mind when I think of her. She was mad at the world and retreated in silence. I wonder if her mouth got twisted from the effort of holding back the angry words.

I know my mom was pretty, once. There were days when flashes of it still showed. When she felt good and could laugh you could see it—the young woman that had existed before all the bitterness and pain had set her mouth and her silence.

She was a good cook, and Dad would bring folks home to show off her cooking; or he'd take things into work she'd baked and have everybody asking for the recipe. My dad was proud of her in many ways, whether she talked or not. There wasn't anything my mom couldn't do with a piece of cloth. She could just look at the dresses in the store windows or magazines, cut a pattern from newspapers, stay up much of the night sewing, and the next day I had a stunning new prom dress. She was very talented; and none of that talent ever got recognized in any way our society prizes. Raising a family and making a dress for your daughter's dance were ordinary things to do in a country home.

More than most people, my mother needed special recognition. She had a need to be set apart in some way. She never got it, and all her life she was angry about that. Being loved by her family simply wasn't enough, and I can understand that. If she had lived at a later age and had a career, perhaps the smile would have come back to her face. For weeks on end my mother didn't speak to my father and I never knew why.

Momma was selfish, too, selfish beyond belief. When I was young, that always embarrassed me. Once, when one of my mom's sisters was dying with cancer, another sister came to visit, bringing the ill sister a new robe. My mom was furious because my aunt had not brought her a robe as well. Not only was my mom not ill, she owned several robes and had more money than others in her family. After the sick sister died, my mom went into the dead sister's closet and took that robe commenting, "See? I got it anyway." It was painful to witness the depth of her need.

MY DAD

My father's job required shift work, so much of my childhood was shrouded in *shhh*s softly whispered by my mother as she held her right index finger perpendicular to her lips. Every night at dusk, Mother would round up Jessica and me and send us to the roof of the barn. She would have spent the day trying to keep us quiet. By nighttime she was sick of the effort. Occasionally, Jessica was allowed to stay in her room and read, but not me, not ever. I was considered too noisy, the troublemaker. It's true. I did fidget, and sitting still for long periods of time was not my strong suit. Trouble—well, it seemed more like trouble found me. If we stayed up on the barn, Mother knew where we were and she didn't have to keep telling us to be quiet.

    Our reward for staying outside was to get a snack with Dad before he left for work at 9:00 p.m. I can still remember the smell of bacon frying for BLTs as I sat on the peak of that tin roof, with the moon overhead and the back pasture stretching as far as I could see. In the foreground there was a pond with a huge live oak tree at the water's edge. I couldn't see the dock, but I knew our raft floated there with its poles still stuck in the mud. In the distance I could see the row of catalpa trees that lined the ditch where we swam when its shallow banks were flooded by rain. Our mother would call, and in we'd rush to join Dad around the white, enamel-topped kitchen table with the straight-backed chairs covered in brown-and-white cowhide. Being there late at night on a summer evening, Jessica and me at the table with Daddy while my mother was preparing his lunch pail, was special. Most other kids had been inside since dark and certainly were in bed by this late hour. It seemed exotic to me to be going off to work late at night while other people prepared things for you.

Except when he went to church, my father always wore khaki pants and insisted on a shirt with two pockets. He parted his smooth black hair down the middle and combed it to either side. His ears were large but close against his head, so you didn't notice. He had a straight, aquiline nose and a strongly defined chin, which gave him an attractive profile. He was tall, but so was everybody in my house, except me. He had a ruddy complexion and brown eyes that my sister inherited. He had a mole on the back of his neck. I had one, just like it, in exactly the same place.

My father was different. People came from miles around just to sit at the back of the house and listen to my father, although they often had to wait a while to hear what he thought about something. He had some pretty wise things to say, but he used words sparingly. You had to listen close if you wanted to know what he thought. He seemed content, my father. I think people came to discover his sense of peace. He was at peace, not only with himself but also with his Maker and his world. I'm not sure how he got it, this peace. It was difficult to be peaceful with my mother around.

He saw us off to school the first day of every year, and he always said the same thing about how we were starting with a clean slate and could make this year whatever we wanted it to be. Somehow, we got the message that we controlled our future and had a choice in how it turned out. My mother was Presbyterian, and visiting her church I learned about predestination. They always talked about how we were like a bird in a cage. Small as I was, I understood they believed possibilities were limited and certain things were bound to be. I liked my dad's philosophy better. He went to the Presbyterian church with my mother, but in his heart he was a Southern Baptist. My mother didn't think that the Baptist religion was dignified enough for her. Southern Baptists were doers, active. Their activity was attractive to me. I never could stand to wait, to be acted upon rather than to act. If there really was such a thing as salvation, I wanted to know I could earn it for myself by my good works. I wanted to think I had some control.

Whenever Daddy talked about that clean slate, I knew his analogy was not quite accurate, because the same four teachers were back every year at our small school and there was a lot already on my slate carried over from the year before—little things, like being put in the cloakroom for catching flies. Flies were dirty, carried disease and germs, and hadn't I listened to the science lecture? I was setting a bad example. The teachers gave me credit for having more influence than I did. I got blamed for being the leader in any kind of trouble. I was just curious. And when I threw Lester over the desk, he deserved it. He was taunting me.

My dad was never idle. When he sat, he sat at the back of the house, either on the screened-in porch, in the yard, or the barn. He sat with his feet wide apart, his elbows on his knees. Resting there, bent over, he peeled pecans, whittled, or repaired a piece of equipment. I never saw my dad when he wasn't busy. I didn't know then that he couldn't sit still; but, because he never hurried, he didn't appear especially busy either.

He raised a large garden every year, far more than our small family could use. He believed, taught us, showed us by example that we were our brother's keeper, and every year he fed people from that garden. Not only did he plant it, till the ground, fertilize it, weed and hoe, he picked the crop. Then, with me climbing in beside him, together we delivered the produce to whoever was less fortunate. Never in any condescending way, it was biblical. The receiver never questioned that my father was simply an instrument of God to feed his flock. People loved my dad, revered him.

It wasn't just the food either. It was labor, whatever neighbors needed. Not so much financially, but rather with sweat and time, he was there to help. Every week he slowly drove the tractor, a journey of forty-five minutes, down the gravel road to the church to mow the four-acre lawn. It was his contribution to the community. He didn't even belong to that church. When he retired, my father stopped in Mr. Sam's carpentry shop every morning to tend the counter for him so Mr. Sam could go by home to check on his crippled daughter. When Sam tried to pay him, my father responded, "I said I needed a job, not a paycheck. Had I wanted money I would have stayed at Standard Oil. Thank you but no." This went on for years.

We had an old black cauldron in the yard that, earlier, had been used to boil clothes. Daddy would fire it up and cook jambalaya for the men of the church on workdays. It took hours, but every ingredient was carefully prepared and chopped by his hands. I can remember the mounds of parsley and the attention to detail that went into the fixin' of that food. The Last Supper wasn't prepared more carefully. Somehow, I learned something about caring for others, just watching him.

Example, I guess that's it. He never talked much about how we should get on in this life or relate to our fellow man, but he lived it. I knew that if I passed this way and had not made a difference, why bother? My life is different because of my father, in good ways and bad. Much later, some part of me would hate him for not protecting me from my mother; but, for now, he was someone I wanted to emulate. I liked the way people felt about him and I liked the way he felt about himself. I wanted to be like that.

My Cathedral

My father never bought anything on credit. So when Jessica and I were little, we lived in rented homes. When I was in the third grade we moved to Ramble Road, right next door to an antebellum home. That home included a long driveway bordered by oak trees where the tips of their branches touched the ground. Mary, the girl who lived in that house, and I spent many a day under, or in, those branches. She was a year younger than I, but an adventurous little girl regardless of her delicate appearance, and would go with me anywhere. On balance, if we stayed home her grandmother served us a tea party on the side screened porch of their home—one half of a Delaware Punch and a cookie.

Behind the house was a huge barn with many stables. Upstairs was a hayloft we played in for hours with the hay sticking to our hot, sweaty bodies. Behind the barn were corrals and cattle chutes for dipping cattle, and on those days two cowboys riding herd as Mary and I perched on the boarded chute, legs intertwined with boards to keep us from falling as we watched the cattle going through. As dark approached the cowboys would come and lift us from the top board, placing us on the ground and saying, "It's time for supper." Dipping time for cattle was an exciting time for us.

Every Saturday morning our mothers gave us twenty-five cents each, and Mary and I walked to the grocery store to buy ground hamburger meat and two potatoes. We both had horses and, along with an iron skillet tied to the saddle, we left for the day. We had many acres to roam, but we always ended up by noon at a huge round tree stump that served as our table. We built a fire and cooked our hamburgers, then cut up our potatoes in small slices so they would cook more quickly. It was a weekly ritual of freedom. For years I had begged and prayed for a horse and now I had one. Long ago I had been shut out of my family, so no one cared where I was. I learned very early how to take care of myself.

There was a pond just outside the fence to the field and every summer we built a new raft. None ever floated but we could pole them across the pond, while being several inches under water.

Mrs. Lettie, an African-American woman, lived in that field, and after supper if it was not a night when I had to go to the top of the barn, I would go talk to Mrs. Lettie. She would be on her porch in a rocker, and I would face her with my bare feet placed between the slats on the railing. Leaning over and holding on to the top railing, we would visit. My mother explained I need not address her as Ma'am—as in *yes, ma'am* or *no, ma'am*—but I ignored my mother. To my mind Mrs. Lettie was an adult and deserved that respect.

Mrs. Lettie had a son, Nathaniel. He played with all of us when we were little, even football. But when I reached puberty, he disappeared. I never knew why. I saw him once, years later downtown, washing store windows. Before I left the South I would come to understand why I never saw him again.

I only had access to my father outdoors. He always said God must not have thought him capable of raising sons because he never gave him one. I became that boy he wanted so badly. Before I was born, my mom had lost a son to stillbirth.

I learned to shoot a rifle. And later, when Dad could pay cash and we moved to our own home on a river, I learned to read the river and knew exactly when there was a log just under the surface of the water. If I sheared a cotter pin, I could quickly change it and keep going. I fished with my dad, running trotlines late at night.

I was not wanted in my home and I knew it, so I spent as much time out-of-doors as possible. It became my cathedral. I learned to love nature. It was my shelter and place of peace. It still is.

MASSACHUSETTS

Robert Harris

1987

The operator's voice came across clearly with only the softest tinge of a Southern accent. "Tulane University."

"Alumni Office, please." Then the quick response, "Alumni Office."

"Yes, good morning. I'm calling for some information. I'm at Smith College in Northampton, Massachusetts, and I'm trying to track down one of your alumni. I was wondering if you could give me their name, address, and phone number. And, if not, if I send a letter to your office, could you forward it to him?"

"Well, if he's listed in the directory we can give it to you, but otherwise no. Where did you say you were from?"

"Smith College."

"Just a minute, let me check. Now, what is the name?"

"Robert Harris. I know he's in California but I don't know where. He owns his own computer company, I know that."

"Just a minute, let me see. Yes, here he is. He's listed in the directory, both his business and his home, so I can give you both, but we have no new information on him since 1985."

"I'm sure he's still there. That'll be fine. Thank you." I couldn't believe it. My heart was pounding, my mouth dry.

"It's Robert P. Harris, Command Computer, Inc." She gave me both his home and business address, and phone number. I mumbled my thanks and appreciation, and hung up the phone.

I stared in disbelief. Here on this sheet of paper, right before my very eyes were the whereabouts of the man I had longed for, for thirty-five years. I could not believe my good fortune. Why hadn't I thought of this before? Why had it taken me thirty-five years to get the courage to try to find him? Not that I hadn't tried before—I had. But they had been half-hearted, minimal efforts, either by looking in phone books at libraries or endeavoring to wheedle some small bit of information from some family member of his I might run into every five or six years. Later I'd think, Why now? But for the moment I wanted to relish the fact that of all the men in the world, I now knew where Robert was. I knew where he lived and all I had to do was pick up the phone.

I focused on the paper before me. It was too early to call. California was three hours behind East Coast time. I'd have to wait.

At exactly 12:30, East Coast time, I picked up the phone and dialed his business number.

"Command Computer."

"Mr. Robert Harris, please."

"Just one moment."

"Rob Harris's office. May I help you?"

"Rob Harris, please."

"May I tell him who's calling?"

"Jasmine Carrietté."

"Just a moment." The moments seemed interminable. Would I be able to speak once I reached him?

"Jazz?"

"Yes."

"I can't believe it. Where are you? How did you find me?"

"Rob, I'm just calling to ask if it's okay to write to you. I wanted to call first to be sure it was okay, that it was safe, that I could be sure it would be you and you alone who would receive or open the letter." I was shaking. My voice cracked and the tears were starting.

His response came slowly and was drawn out, "Holy moley." Here was a phrase from the fifties. There was a long silence. Was he unchanged since then?

"Rob, are you okay?"

He cleared his throat. "Yeah."

"Rob, I realize I knew I was going to call and you didn't. This must be hitting you really hard. It'll take some time to adjust."

"How did you find me?"

"I called the Alumni Office at Tulane."

"I'd have never thought of that."

"Neither did I all these years."

"Where are you?"

"In Massachusetts. I'm at Smith College in Northampton. Would you like my phone number in case you go into shock later?"

"Yes, let me have it. I was in the Boston area last fall."

"It's xxx-xxxx, area code xxx."

"I'll probably wait until I hear from you."

"Rob, how has life treated you?"

"It could have been better."

"I guess we all could say that."

"What a morning."

"Rob, you have two children, don't you?"

"Yes, the traditional one of each."

"Well, you'll hear from me within a few days."

"I'm sorry I can't talk. What a morning."

"All I wanted was to be sure it was safe to write. I don't want to keep you. You'll hear from me soon."

I placed the telephone back in the receiver and went to my typewriter. I owed this man an explanation. It had taken me thirty-five years to be able to call him. An apology was long overdue. It was a gift I wanted him to have, this explanation and my love. I could tell from the conversation he was stunned at my reappearance. Well, why not?

Jasmine Carrietté

April 22, 1987

Dear Rob,

How strange, after all these years, to be talking to you. The twisting and turnings, the miles, the experiences that finally brought me to place the call to you this morning are too numerous to outline in this initial letter. I'll save those details and gradually fill you in on where I've been and what I've been doing over the last thirty-five years. I want to begin right now exactly where we left off; was it in the fall of 1952?

From this perspective, I cannot believe how intuitively bright you were then, how advanced in wisdom for your years. You knew, could see, so much more clearly than I. I have always been grateful for your persistence and tenacity in trying to stop me from making the biggest mistake of my life. I wish you had known then the odds you were fighting; for if you had, I have no doubt your skill would have overcome them. Ignorance on my part and a reticence to talk about real issues led to my ultimate downfall. I was too young, too afraid, too desirous of pleasing my parents, etcetera—all of the negative things youth endows us with. Enough apologies for my ignorance. Let me get to the explanation.

Do you recall confronting me once about thinking you had overheard me "making out" with some boy in a car one night during a dance at my school? I wouldn't be surprised if you do not recall it, but nevertheless you did—confront me, that is. It never happened. Not only had I never had sex with anyone, I had not been in any parked car either. Your accusation hurt me terribly, and I did not feel I had convinced you that I had not indeed been in that car. I had no way to prove it was not me. You made me feel so guilty and I had done nothing. I felt you did not trust me. Later, when you asked me to wait for you to finish school, I felt so unsure.

Rob, can you know how ignorant I was about sex? God, it seems incomprehensible to me now. I believe I had touched your phallus once, through your clothing. You had placed my hand there. I can recall to this day the size and feel of you and the response you aroused in me.

I remember, too, you said to me, "Do you think you can handle it?" And my reply of, "I'd like to try." I recall the guilt I felt about such an unabashed statement on my part, but that was exactly what I felt. I was dying to be with you, intimately. I remember once, very briefly, sitting across you in the car and the terrible guilt that engulfed me all the next week at how unbelievably forward I had been, to straddle you like that. I could not know at that age and in those days how much the hormones were raging, and how perfectly natural it was to feel the way I felt about you, yet all I felt was guilt. Then, when you questioned me about the incident when you thought you overheard me in a car with some other man, I felt—because I desired you so much and allowed you to take liberties that I allowed no one else—why shouldn't you question my ability to control my feelings. Regardless of how much I was taught about "saving myself for my husband," I was then and remain to this day a woman who enjoys a level of sexual desire I seldom witness in others. That desire had, of course, led me to masturbate, so I knew my own body pretty well. The entire mystique surrounding the hymen was certainly a part of my sexual folklore. I touched myself often and did not feel it. Where was it? Did I have a hymen? Was it missing? Did horseback riding really deflower young virgins? What if? What if I did not have one? What if there was no proof I was a virgin? You had already questioned my virginity and I knew I had done nothing wrong; yet, what if I married you? On our wedding night when there was no blood visible, would you divorce me? I was terrified. It was not something I could talk to anyone about. Up until then, the worst problem I had ever faced was my brother-in-law giving me a brassiere for Christmas because he had a crush on me. You solved that problem for me, remember?

You were my best friend, but now you were the one questioning me. I was afraid, but could not talk to you about it. I never talked to my mother about anything and certainly could not go to her with this. I can understand now, from this distance, that this seems like a nonissue. To a nineteen-year-old Southern girl in the 1950s, virginity was everything. I was a virgin. I thought I had no proof for you. I did, of course. There was blood on the sheets on my wedding night (which only makes the story more tragic), but from my own self-examination I could not tell. I thought I would be the biggest disappointment of your life. You would hate me. You would divorce me because you would believe I was "damaged goods." I thought we would begin a life where you felt you could place no trust in me. I thought by refusing to be involved with you I was saving us both, me from humiliation, and you from a life with a woman you would always believe had betrayed you. Even writing this now, all these years later, I grieve that such tragic ignorance could entirely change the direction and course of my life and my chance for happiness. I do believe, have always believed, that had I married you my life would have been happy in ways indiscernible to me—mainly, because of your mind. I'll elaborate on that at another time.

The other issue, separate but important, was my mother's feelings about your family. Although my mom was friends with your mother, in fact until my mother's death, my mother was very insecure because your family had money and mine did not. Mother was especially uncomfortable that you would have a college education and I would not. Over and over she kept hammering home to me the fact that I would always feel uncomfortable and insecure because you came from money and were educated, and I possessed neither of those things. When in point of fact, she felt insecure. I was too young and too stupid to realize or to care about either. I simply loved you. That love, plus the irony that, years later, I discover I am anything but dumb (I can't imagine you being attracted to somebody dumb) is another tragedy. My mother was relentless.

In addition, all of my life I had sought my parents' approval and never got it. That's one of the reasons I rebelled so. They adored Allen. He hunted and fished with my father. He was the son they had always wanted. They did not feel threatened by him as they did by you. Allen was a good ole boy. Finally, I married Allen to please my parents. It seems trite to say it, but Allen and I should have never been together. Allen is a good person. I nearly ruined his life. He deserved someone quiet and sweet. I am neither. Well, at least not quiet.

I remember a friend of ours from school telling me years later that she told you to leave me alone, to forget it, to let it go. I wanted to scream. I thought if you had pushed a little harder, perhaps I would have broken down and told you my terrible dark secret about my fear regarding proof of my virginity and thus leave the decision up to you. But finally, you stopped pushing and the next step in my life was inevitable.

In retrospect, as I've looked back on the experience of you trying to reason with me, arguing with me, about marrying you rather than Allen, coming to my house to confront me, calling, trying to reason with my parents, I've always marveled at the courage you had to fight for me, for what you wanted. I knew you possessed those qualities. I had watched you in action with others, getting what you wanted. I admired you for it. I still do. You were essentially standing up for my right to be happy. Few people have ever done that for me. It made me feel special and loved and that you cared enough about me to endeavor to keep me from ruining my life. I love you for that.

I wish you had succeeded, but you could never have known such foolish things were ruling the decision-making process, and who knows, even had you known they may not have seemed foolish to you at the age of twenty. You treated me with such respect sexually. God, now that I know what young men go through at that age, I cannot believe your self-control; but that kind of control would have demanded it of me as well. I had it but thought I had no proof, and I was already being questioned. Rob, can you remember the guilt we felt about anything sexual?

One of the things my work here at Smith is about, is desire. Women are taught to have the perfect Madison Avenue body, to be found desirable, to attract men, but the issue of a woman desiring is seldom discussed. I do desire, discuss, and act. I do to a degree many women don't—to a degree few men do. I think always you knew this about me. I never acted on it but I felt it, still do. I remember one afternoon sitting in my living room when I lived on Tiger Bend Road, and can even remember the dress I had on at the time. You were sitting across from me and said something about your fantasy of me and what it would be like, and someday the fulfillment of that fantasy. I didn't even know what you were referring to then, but through the years I've imagined it. Desire—as a young girl how often I lay at night in the field next to our house, gazing up at the stars, and cried because I loved you, wondering what you were doing and grateful that at least the same galaxy encompassed us, and I felt close to you until the morning came and I could see you again. Coming to terms with my own sexuality has been a lifelong struggle.

Through the years, no one in your family has been willing to talk to me about you. Intuitively, I think they knew I still loved you and, protecting you and your happiness, did not want me to be able to contact you. They needn't have worried, only with age have I gained the courage.

I have written all my life, but never showed my work to anyone until three years ago. Since that time, I have been on fellowships at Radcliffe, Cambridge University in England, and currently, here at Smith. I am an Ada Comstock Scholar, a wonderful program for nontraditional students, which allows women whose education was interrupted, for one reason or another, to return to school. I will be here another year. One of the things I've discovered by being at these schools is that I have talent. It has taken me fifty years to know. If I had married you originally, my entire life would have been different. You had the intelligence to deal with me. I grieve for us both, for the joy we may have shared. I'm writing to say I loved you then; I have loved you all of my life; I love you still. I wanted you to know that before I died. I did not want to leave this earth with you not knowing. I wanted you to know what fantasies I have had of you through the years. You would have engaged my energies, and they were many. You would have connected with me on an intellectual and physical level I've never yet realized. All of my life I feel I have been searching for what I had with you. I withdrew from three other relationships. I am not so naïve as to believe we are the same people we were at twenty. We have grown in separate ways, and had we the chance to be together might have nothing in common, may hate each other or even—God forbid—be sexually incompatible but . . . the dream never faded. Today I still love the man I knew you to be.

I want to keep in touch with you. If the chance arises, I hope someday to see you again. You are not free to respond to me as you were at the age of twenty, and please know I have no desire to disrupt your life. This contact was not made with that intention. I don't mean to be presuming either that I could disrupt it. I am just saying that now that I've found you after all these years, will you please allow me to write or call occasionally if it causes no problem for you? And I hope you will be willing to do the same.

I love you, Rob. I hope you will call me sometime and bring me up to date on where you are in life and what you are feeling in response to all of this. Did you, too, still love me for a while? Have you thought of me ever in these intervening years? What? Is this all my fantasy and imagination? Did you ever love me or did I make all of this up? Have the years clouded my memory? Is this only my perception of what happened? I cannot know your reaction. I haven't a clue to what you are feeling or how you might respond, except your comment on the phone that had you known where I was in the Boston area, you would have seen me last fall. You've been married to the same woman for years, not the unstable life I've lived—searching, questing, for what? A memory? My only clue that all is not paradise is your comment of Wednesday, "It (i.e., life) could have been better" . . . which parts? Talk to me. Strange, I think I have the right to ask.

I love you—I always have,

Jazz

My current address on Smith campus is:
Jasmine Carrietté
10 Prospect Street
Northampton, Massachusetts 01063
Phone number: xxx/xxx-xxxxx

Should you need time to absorb all of this before you respond, I'll be alone at the beach from May 9 to May 30. My address and phone number there are: 374 E. Yacht Drive, Long Beach, North Carolina 28461 xxx/xxx-xxxx

Jasmine Carrietté

May 19, 1987
Long Beach, North Carolina

Memories, what memories. I'd thought of him so often during all the long years since we'd last spoken. Rob and I grew up together, across the street from one another. Although she was younger, his sister Beth had been my friend, too. I had loved him for as long as I could remember. And then things had gone wrong, terribly wrong, but not because of him. I remembered how brave he had been. At nineteen, Robert had more courage than any man I ever knew. He fought to win and keep and have me for his wife at an age and in a time when others would not have had the courage to face the opposition he did—not only from me because of my fear, but from my parents as well. The memory of his courage had nurtured an image of him in my mind that was probably out of all proportion to reality. Fantasy, what an exciting fantasy life I had. It helped to dull the pain. How real is Robert to me? I would soon find out.

I was house-sitting for my friend June, who was in Saint John visiting her daughter, when Robert called.

"Hello."

"Jazz, this is Robert."

"Oh my God! Rob, I'm . . . so glad you could call. I wasn't sure I'd ever hear from you. I know the courage it took for you to place this call, because I know the courage it took for me to place that first call to you and write to you. I appreciate you being willing to be in touch."

"Well, you're right about the courage. I feel like a philanderer just placing this call. I don't mean this in any negative way, but you have to understand, you're like, dead to me. It's . . . you're like a ghost come back from the grave. You'll never know what I went through." Rob's voice faltered and I could tell he was having difficulty speaking. "I tried to bury you. I spent years trying to bury you. And then your call, and everything must have been right under the surface, because there you were in full force right before me. I still don't understand. Why now? I don't want to make you feel bad and I'm not judging you, but what went wrong?"

"It's okay, you're not making me feel bad, and of course you're going to have lots of questions. I'll try to answer them for you but it'll take a while. I'll write."

"You asked about me. Would you like for me to bring you up to date on me? I talk better than I write."

"Sure."

"Well, after finishing school I went to work at General Electric in New Orleans."

"Oh, you stayed in New Orleans. I didn't know that."

"Yes, then I transferred to their corporate headquarters in Metairie and that's where I met my wife, Beverly. She was in the marketing department. We got married in '55 and moved out here to Carmel. Let me see . . . I worked for someone else for about five years and then I started my own business. So I've been in business for myself for twenty-seven years. I just recently hired additional top management so I can get more time off and be less involved in day-to-day operations."

"Great. Don't you like running your own business? Outside of sex there's nothing more exciting. In fact, it might be a close tie. I owned my own business, too, but not on such a grand scale."

Laughing with recognition, "Really, what?"

"I was Senior Sales Director with a cosmetics company. There is no high in the world like building something from scratch that never existed before. Doing it used all of my assets to best advantage. I loved it."

"You'll have to tell me more about that."

"I will, but for now I'm catching up on you."

"Let me see. My wife, I've never talked to another woman about my wife. It seems strange. Does it bother you?"

"No. I know you're married, Rob."

"I've liked being married. I've liked that there's someone here when I come home."

"I'd like that, too. We're just not all that fortunate."

"I know. I'm sorry."

"You needn't be. You needn't apologize that you managed your life well and got what you wanted."

"Well, not everything."

Silence. We left it there.

I knew, could tell, he felt uncomfortable. So much was being left unsaid. We tiptoed around each other's feelings. Me, with my impulsive nature straining to hold back my protestation of love, affection, and gratitude that he had called, and he feeling overwhelmed with guilt for calling. His first infidelity in thirty-two years of marriage, yet I could hear the emotion in his voice, the being glad to hear my voice, to talk to me, to know I was alive.

"Jazz, when I was in Boston last fall I knew you were somewhere in the area. I looked for your face in every crowd. I wish I could have seen you."

"Oh, Rob, it's so good just to know where you are in this world."

"Jazz, don't ever come out here. Don't just show up on my doorstep. I couldn't handle that. It's going to take me a long time to absorb all of this. I don't know, am I going through some kind of midlife crisis or something?"

"Can a midlife crisis come from outside yourself? I called you, remember?"

"I don't know, but I've given it considerable thought and I've made a conscious decision. I want to stay in touch."

We were both crying at this point. It had taken him nearly a month to come to this decision and respond to my letter. I could sense his struggle with the decision to deceive his wife for the first time in all their years together. It was a conscious choice and one he didn't feel good about. That was obvious. I'm not sure how freely the choice was made. At fifty-five, there isn't much time left for dreaming. First loves are such illusive, gossamer things. You'd need to be superhuman to purposely let go of a dream at this age. The very quality which made him so attractive to me was causing him a lot of pain.

"I'm glad you're able to keep in touch, Rob. That's wonderful. That's more than I could have ever expected or hoped for. I'll answer your questions, and will certainly keep in touch and let you know where I am, when I'm moving, and where I'm going."

"Please do."

We said our good-byes.

I hung up the phone and burst into tears. I had taken such a risk. I kept saying to myself it didn't matter if I never heard from him, that

Desire Makes the Difference

I had done what I needed to do. But I was obviously lying. It mattered a great deal that he was able to respond. I was grateful he could and I knew what it cost him. Moral principles were everything to Rob and this phone call changed how he viewed himself. I didn't want to be a part of his unhappiness. What a dilemma; but for now, I just wanted to rejoice in the reestablishment of the best relationship I had ever had with a man.

Long Beach, the island I was on, was nearly deserted, so I had plenty of time to walk on the beach and think. For the rest of that day, memories of my childhood with Rob came flooding back. I felt as though I was overwhelmed and drowning in memories, so many memories, like the day he used a pulley to hoist my bicycle to the very top of an enormous oak tree. I searched for days for that bike. Who would ever think to look up? For the rest of my life I'd search for men who proved their attraction in such dramatic ways. I remembered walking across the blacktop street on my heels, barefoot, to his house on ninety-eight-degree summer days and how the hot tar would stick and burn. Yes, I'd still walk over hot tar to get to Rob.

I got out June's portable typewriter to compose my second letter to this glorious man.

Jasmine Carrietté

May 20, 1987

Dear Rob,

I wish I was at home so I could get onto paper more readily what is in my head and my heart. At home I have a word processor; here, a portable noncorrecting typewriter. Bear with me through this messy letter and I promise a better one when I return to Massachusetts.

First and foremost, I want to say how glad I am that you could call me. You must realize that for the past month I have had no clue as to your reaction. Was it positive you were recovering from the shock? Were you repulsed by the whole display of emotion? Did you feel it was all the fantasy of a middle-aged woman? What? I would have never known had you been unable to call. Thank you for letting me know your reaction.

Beyond that, what is it I am feeling? Primarily grateful, grateful to know where you are, what you are doing, and that you are well. I'm glad also to know that all these years my love was not based on fantasy alone but that you, too, feel some response to me. That is enough, quite enough. Were I younger it would not be, but at this age and at this time in my life, it is enough. I am so glad I've finally found you and that you can be a good, healthy part of my life again. We will keep it just this way.

Let me reassure you once more. I would never appear on your doorstep unannounced. I was horrified you even thought I might, but glad you expressed your fear so I could reassure you. Remember, I called you to be certain it was safe to write. Your willingness to be in touch occasionally is an extra. My reason for writing was to correct an old wrong, truly a tragedy as I see it. Not only was my entire life affected by such a grievous mistake—you never had a chance to know. You lived your life believing I had freely chosen someone else over you, when nothing could have been further from the truth. I wanted to correct that mistake. That is all. The fact that you can and will communicate with me is a plus; a wonderful, unexpected plus for which I am grateful. But were it not possible for you to continue, I've done what I needed to do. You know I love you, always have and always will.

I must, however, stress one other point so you will understand. Since you don't know the person I've become, try to base your trust in me on that person you knew earlier, years ago. Base your trust in me on the values you know I was raised with and time will justify your trust. Rob, I want you to not be frightened that I desire you. I cannot be in any relationship that denies the healthy, good, vibrant, physical part of myself. For too many years that part of me was denied, pushed down, restrained, and subdued. For eleven years I was married to a man who never once touched my breasts. Never again will anyone make me feel guilty about the physical part of myself. Hear me loud and clear: I will never act on that desire. You don't know me yet well enough to know how strongly I feel about women. I am so phallically oriented I will never be a lesbian, but I feel so strongly that women are so bright, able, and heroic. I feel strongly about women's rights.

I have been single almost twelve years. I have never dated married men. I cannot deny I desire you. I do. I've fantasized about you for years with little physical exploration of one another to lend much credibility to those fantasies, but I would never do anything to risk your marriage or make any implication that could harm your wife or children in any way. That is not what I seek, nor is it something I would ever want on my conscience. No matter what we might feel for one another it cannot discount responsibility, nor can it ever replace raising a family with a woman you love. I would not personally want the burden or the guilt of that, but I can love you, and that includes the physical, even if only in my mind, okay? Fantasies are wonderful. Allow me to express them. I will not act them out. Desire is glorious. Don't make me feel guilty for having it. Trust my goodness and honesty. I will never arrive on your doorstep. Although sexual intimacy may never be a part of our relationship, I feel that yesterday was the culmination of a thirty-five-year intercourse, a dialog inside my mind, and only now is the partner real.

There is so much I want to say. I wish we could sit for three days and nights and talk, catch up, share, who we are and where we've been. I'm pretty verbal, but bringing you up to date on thirty-five years and the experiences that shaped my character and made me who I am will take a while.

This next year will find me involved in my major life's work. It is very gratifying that you will be here to share this experience with me.

All day yesterday, after your call, my mind was filled with you. What a marvelous reunion. Welcome home, welcome home to me. I've missed you, your intelligence, your body, I've longed for you forever—I'm glad to know you're there.

I love you,

Jasmine

There is so much I want to say but this typewriter is such an unbelievable pain. No one can read my handwriting, so I will write again when I have access to better equipment.

May 27, 1987
Long Beach, North Carolina
Rob called again right after he received my letter.

"Jazz, I wanted to clear something up. I don't want to just be in touch occasionally. I want to know everything. Where you've been, what you've done, what went wrong, and I also want to know, why now? Why after all these years? Don't get me wrong, I'm glad, I'm glad you called, but why did it take you thirty-five years?"

Laughing, "I'll do my best to answer all your questions but it'll take a while. I can't explain a lifetime in a few brief sentences."

"Another thing, Jazz, you'll hear from me often."

It was hard to respond. "You know, Rob, when I wrote that first letter it was something I had to do. I guess I never gave a lot of thought to follow-up responses, what I might feel if you responded favorably, and the impact that might have on me. I was sort of unprepared for all I've been feeling. You, too?"

"Oh, what an understatement. I don't know what's happening to me."

"In 1980, I knew you were still married because I saw your mother when my mom died, and knowing you, I figured you were still married. So I just never considered much beyond explaining what had happened and maybe being forgiven. But to hear you say you'll be in touch often is overwhelming to me. I know that costs you something. I'm grateful. I love being able to talk to you."

"I don't understand it yet. I just know that I want to know everything about you."

"You will."

"Write me. Write soon."

And so began our course in unchartered waters. Drifting back in time, we began to dissolve into one another again, to merge, in a way that both pleasured and frightened us.

Jasmine Carrietté

June 1, 1987

Dear Rob,

What a very pleasant surprise to hear from you again so soon. Thank you for the call. I apologize for the shock I must have caused you by reappearing after all these years, but I cannot think of any way I might have approached you which would not have been a shock. Take as long as you need to recover and realize I am not a ghost.

I'm trying to think of the best way to begin to answer some of your questions, especially your question about "Why now?" I believe in great part my ability to finally reach out to you was precipitated by my age and my work. I have recently come to terms with many issues in my life. Finally, the one thing left unresolved was my earlier relationship to you. Putting some closure on that relationship, acknowledging the loss of you, grieving over it, really facing the grief I'd always felt about it was an important thing for me to do. That, and telling you about it, reaffirming my love for you and verbalizing it to you was something I needed to do. I wanted you to know. That was part of the impetus for contacting you. The other pertinent factor was my writing. For that explanation, I'll need to go further back in time.

Between Christmas and New Year's of 1983, I made up my mind I was going to make some major changes in my life. I was fifty years old. I knew I would need help to do that, and in January of 1984 I entered a year of intensive therapy with a very fine woman named Lilly Foster. Together, we literally changed my life. One decision included, finally, after years of writing, to allow someone capable of judging to read my work. Previously I had written from a need to express myself, with never any thought of publication. I had to write, but I certainly did not see my work as exceptional or especially worthy of sharing. I had no need to share it. Over the years friends had commented about my letters to them, and I thought their praise was because they loved me, not because I was an especially good writer. Shortly after Christmas of 1983, I had lunch with a man and his wife who were involved in the publishing industry. I had known them through business connections.

I gave them a sample of my writing and asked if they would read it and give me their opinion. He called a week later to say, "You write about universal issues in ways I've never seen expressed before. My wife and I fought over who got to read first. We were riveted, involved. You were writing about us. Yes, you have the gift." He encouraged me to pursue publication and offered his assistance.

I then submitted a sample of my writing to the Radcliffe Seminars Program, which was offering a writing seminar limited to fifteen people. I was accepted, and on the first day of class the professor asked if I could stay after for a few minutes to talk to him. I did and he said, "You absolutely and unquestionably can write. You absolutely and unquestionably can be published."

As I told you over the telephone, one of the reasons I hesitated to show my work to anyone is because it is highly sexual. This makes me feel very vulnerable, and a writer feels vulnerable enough without the sexual issue. His comment was, "You do not write about sex. You write about giving, and loss, and sex, and death, and self-abnegation, and self-oblivion." I knew I had communicated. I lost my fear of being published. Of course, there will be those who look at my work for sexual reasons, but there will be people who see beyond the sex to the real message I'm striving to convey. I decided to pursue it. Publication would allow me to reach far more women than I could ever reach in my cosmetic business. Radcliffe offered me a scholarship just to write and encouraged me to apply for a Bunting fellowship, which I still may do after I finish here at Smith. With the newfound validation about my writing, I decided to look around and see who would offer me the most financial support and the best environment to work in. I made the decision to come to Smith but still keep my contact with Radcliffe.

My Scholars committee here at Smith believes my work has profound implications, not only for women but for men as well. At Gonville and Cauis College at Cambridge University last summer, one don wrote on my term paper, "Simply a tour de force." Academic backing gives my work the credibility I seek. Smith believes I have a blockbuster on my hands. I say all of this for one reason. Gradually, over the past three years, I have heard repeatedly how successful they expect my work to be. You must know that I do not see myself in that light, and of course they could be very wrong and none of this may ever happen, but I also began to think, as I looked over my life, two things: One, my connection to you was left incomplete and I wanted to complete that circle. And two, they say that I will be financially successful because I will be successful on the talk shows. Few writers make a living writing. They believe because I am so verbal, so quotable, so direct, frank, and open, that I will be a big success on television. Repeatedly, I had visions of you seeing me on some talk show, buying my book, and reading it. That way, you would have only been reading about the consequences of my not marrying you, but you would never have known WHY I made the decision I did. I did not ever want that to happen. Of course, none of the above may ever happen, but had I looked you up AFTER it had happened I am not sure you would have believed me. If I was going to contact you then, I had to do it now rather than after the fact. Does that make any sense at all to you? Perhaps it will after you've read my work. I hope so. All of this may be perfectly meaningless to you at this point in time since so much of my reasoning is based on my life experiences and what has happened as a result of that fateful decision to marry Allen.

There is so much still to share with you before you will be up to date with where I am, not only in my thinking but simply the physical location of and movements in my life. Granted, my decision to contact you now may indeed be premature if I am basing that decision on my success as a writer, but I felt to endeavor to be in touch after you had read the story of my life would have been fatal to my intent. Much of my reasoning is based on pure conjecture, things that, in reality, may never take place, but since I had always wanted to tell you of my love and what had actually happened, I knew if I was ever going to do it, it had to be before publication, not after. Few writers are ever successful. The odds are a million to one. It was not a chance I was willing to take, given all of the positive feedback I have had about my writing. I screwed things up once with you. I did not want to do it again. I would never have wanted you to read my book and not understand the sequence of events—to know that every other experience in my life was precipitated by that fateful choice so long ago.

Age played a big part in my ability to follow out my instinct to call you. All through the years I've wanted you to know exactly what I wrote to you in my first letter, but I gathered from what little I was able to glean from your family that you were extremely happy and successful, and I had no desire to cause you any problems. For a woman there is something very wonderful about being fifty or over. No longer is she ruled so much by propriety. Finally, I simply went with my feelings and what I needed to do, and worried less about what you might think or how you might react. I knew I had no desire to disrupt your life. I guess, too, I did not feel needy. I knew it was a gift I wanted you to have—the knowledge, that is. I do not need anything in return. That, too, allowed me to call. Coming to you from a place of strength with my love has different implications for both of us.

Another factor, but one which nevertheless had a significant pull for me, is to be connected in some way to people of importance from my life. That certainly includes you. There is almost no one from my early years in the South to whom I can relate. My sister spent a few days with me in North Carolina last month. I cried after she left. I had not seen her in almost three years. I knew we had to build a new relationship because I am a different person than I was five years ago, but there is a gulf that separates us so wide she may as well be on another continent. I do not feel that with you, even though we have had no contact for thirty-five years. So roots, connectedness, is another factor I am sure, although not as strong as the first two.

Enough about that for now, I am tired of delving into reasons. For the moment, I just want to revel in the fact that it has happened. Shall I tell you a little about where I am physically? Don't know about you, but the last few weeks have found me spending much mental energy in imagining your routine day: How you interact with people, where you go, who you see, what you do. Are you smiling, how do you look, and are you, too, thinking of me? It has been hard, hasn't it? God, do the memories come flooding back. I did not know my fantasy life would take such hold. Well, back to where I am.

I arrived at Smith the end of January 1985. I was fifty-two years old. I had owned and lived in my home in Carlisle, Massachusetts for many years, alone. Carlisle is a very small town near Concord. My home was in a beautiful location, but it was so large and I was exhausted from taking care of it by myself all through the years. There were large, terraced gardens and a pond out back, a lovely setting which was difficult for me to give up. But I had to work long hours and travel all the time to keep it, yet I never got to spend much time there. After living with Thomas Trout for three years I knew I would never go back there because, although the location is ideal, I wanted something smaller and easier to care for. I sold my house when I came to Smith. I have an excellent financial advisor on Martha's Vineyard. She is not only incredibly bright and honest, but she understands about being a single female of fifty-four and the financial implications of that. She invests wisely for me, but with less risk than if there were two incomes or I was younger. Although Smith provides marvelous support academically, emotionally, and financially, I have still not worked for the last two and a half years, and that can be scary for someone my age. I could not have done it without Mary Penure watching my assets. Every artist is looking for a roof over their head and the kind of support I have, so I feel fortunate, but it is still a courageous risk I am taking.

Well anyway, I live on campus in a lovely old house. I have the entire first floor. It is a huge apartment, very comfortable, with many windows and lots of light. I have a twenty-six-year-old roommate. She works a full-time and a part-time job, has several boyfriends and goes to school as well, so I seldom see her. We get along well and I like her very much. I spend most of my time in isolation due to my work. The Smith campus is simply lovely. Olmsted did the landscaping, the same man who did Boston's Emerald Necklace, and although landscaped, it is done to look as though it were a natural setting. I enjoy the beauty and the peace of this place very much. Never in my life have I been so nurtured as I have been during my time here. Everyone is here just for MY success or so it seems. My years here have been some of the happiest, most pleasant of my life.

Although sex is one of my most very favorite things, I imagine the fact that these years of being nurtured, coinciding with my years of celibacy, account in no small way for the amount of peace I have felt. Northampton is known as the Greenwich Village of New England and I find it a lovely little town. I walk everywhere. I never have to drive in the snow anymore. The college does all the plowing; they clear all the walks and even sweep my porch. I live in what is known as the Pioneer

Valley. There are five colleges here and about 40,000 students in the valley, yet it is small town. The Berkshires and Tanglewood are nearby. This will be my first summer in the valley. I am using the summer to work on my book.

In my next letter I'll try to send you something that will give you some indication of how other people see me. That should enable you to tell something about my personality. I don't have many pictures, but I will try to have some copies made for you of the most recent ones. I have set extremely unrealistic, high goals for myself for the summer and the amount of work I want to get done. Otherwise, I would just sit and write to you full-time so we could catch up. That is simply not feasible for me at the moment, so I will call you sometime, too. I hope you can find the time to write to me as well.

Robert, your life sounds like a storybook. What could be better? You said on the phone during my first call to you that life could have been better. Would you elaborate on that? What do you feel you would have done differently, if anything? I want to know everything about you, not just the good parts, not just the physical, but also the emotional, the feelings. Please respond, tell me where you are emotionally. I know I was unprepared for the emotional surge of actually being in contact with you. Share with me what you are feeling.

You asked whether I was still beautiful. I do not feel beautiful but people say that I am. I promise you it is not the physical. I believe people are attracted to my energy and zest for life.

I shall endeavor in my next letter to fill you in on some of the earlier years and to answer your questions about "What went wrong?" I am tired. It is late. I'll close for now, but shall probably call to let you know this letter is on the way. Know that I hold you close. I cherish the memory of you and am so very glad you can now be real to me again.

I feel such love and warmth for you.

Jasmine

Jasmine Carrietté

June 3, 1987

Dear Rob,

It is Wednesday, June 3, and I just talked to you about four hours ago. This is the difficult part of a long-distance relationship. Something you said has stayed on my mind and yet it would be inappropriate for me to call you right back to discuss it. Before you receive this note, I shall probably have talked to you about it, but regardless, I am putting it in print because I need to express myself so I can get on with more constructive things, and also, it will probably be good for you to see it in print so you will know just exactly how strongly I feel about it. Robert, it worries me to hear you say things like "Isn't it terrible?" when you refer to thinking about or relating to me. I'm sure you did not mean it in any negative/personal way, but what I am afraid you mean is "Isn't it terrible?" because (being married) you feel you are being unfaithful to your wife. I want the renewal of our knowledge of one another to be a joy, a support, and comfort to BOTH of us. I do not wish for it to bring you grief.

What scares me, since I don't really know the person you have become very well yet, is this: I am afraid you are going to feel so guilty about just thinking of me, or calling me, that you will feel a need to CONFESS. Please, reassure me that is the most remote thing from your mind. I remember you as smarter than that, but you have lived such a straight life you scare me a little. I would not want to be a part of any confession. Your mind is at once both the most and the least you can give me. I want it: I want it very much. But I do not want you (or me) to have to feel guilty if we share that part of ourselves. I felt very good when you called me after my second letter to say you had given it considerable thought and had made a conscious decision to keep in touch, and more than just occasionally. Please reassure me you have no need to confess anything to anyone. I do not feel we have done anything wrong, but if you do that would cause me pain. Okay? Let me know ASAP what you are feeling about this.

Never was my reconnecting intended to cause pain. I am too old for anything but pleasure.

Jazz

June 8, 1987
Journal
I had talked with Rob the night before. I could not share these feelings with him.

My dear man, what is it you have done to my mind? Today, this morning, I am suffused with you, immersed, drowning in memory after memory from so long ago. I recall your hands, strong and sure, which held mine. I remember a Buick you drove and the delightful times we spent on the front seat parked in my driveway. I remember the drives we took across the river after you had disconnected the odometer. I remember hot summer days as a young girl and seeing you with only an undershirt hanging loose outside your pants, and visually, as though you stood before me still, I want to now, with the knowledge of these years, lift your undershirt and feel with my hands your smooth, hard stomach. I remember the slant of your shoulders as you held them so erect and the way your head lifted just slightly so that you led with your chin, facing the world unafraid and questioning. I recall so vividly your presence as though I saw you last night rather than spoke with you. No matter that the years have passed and our bodies no longer look the same, memory puts my hands on your stomach and I see and feel with the eyes of years of loving. I want to feel you. I want to smell your skin near me but I would not stop there. I would undo your belt, place my hands inside your trousers and lower them to the floor. I would kneel before you and explore you in a way none other has. When one has waited for thirty-five years for something, the desire to know increases. God, do I think of you. At our age, I need to know the physical now. Our minds will be there forever. How long will the physical last? Shameless, I'm absolutely shameless. Isn't it incredible that thirty-five years later, nothing has really changed. We still can't touch, and the prohibition against it now is far greater than before. If only we had known.

Fantasies of you are all that I can have, but oh my love, they are glorious. Interesting, isn't it, that it is the cerebral which ignites the physical. It is your love of business, people, books, your goodness (the very quality which denies you to me) that makes me want your body.

Oh Rob, I've loved you for so long. I'm so glad, so very very glad I can finally talk to you.

I don't make things easy, do I? Robert, can you understand that my very first feelings of desire, other than Oedipal, were for you? Can you understand that I have had those feelings of desire and admiration since I was in the third grade? Can you understand how wonderful it is to finally share those feelings with you verbally, even though I cannot share the reality of physical touch?

People have to care about the protagonist of a novel. They have to care enough to keep turning the pages. I had written character sketches for the principals in my book but was having trouble describing myself without feeling narcissistic, so I asked my friend Diana to write down for me how she sees me. I laughed at her description of me. The main character needs to be attractive but not perfect. I certainly don't come out looking perfect, but other friends who have read it say she has captured me exactly. I disagree on only two points. She is wrong about me being more demanding in male relationships. I do not demand nearly enough for myself or I have not in the past. I am changing that. The other thing I disagree with is my change in being pushy that people grow. It is not that I have aged and thus stopped pushing; it is that I am well. I don't need to change the entire world anymore, just myself.

I still plan to write and try to describe to you "What went wrong?" but I spent Tuesday through Thursday in Boston this week, which means I will work the weekend to try to catch up with the schedule I've set for myself. I will also have to go back to Boston next week for about twenty-four hours from Tuesday until Wednesday noon, so that really cuts into my writing schedule. Boston is a two-hour drive from here; therefore, you won't get that explanation until a little later.

Hope all is well with you. Soon, I shall write again.

Love,

Jazz

June 20, 1987

Dearest Rob,

You will never know how relieved I was to get your letter. After sending the short note about things I remembered and my fantasies, I was afraid I had offended you. I'm glad my fears were unfounded.

I shall attempt to respond to some of your questions. By the way, I have begun the letter explaining what went wrong, but it is now four pages long and I have not even gotten through the first marriage. This is going to take a while, so I shall find a suitable stopping place and mail it. I'll do the story in bits and pieces, as I am able to get to it.

Now, to your letter. Did you write to me from New Orleans after I was engaged to Allen? If you did, I do not recall it and I wonder if my mother kept mail from me. Perhaps you were referring to other letters from New Orleans. Robert, you must know how good it was to get your recent letter. To be holding something in my hands which only a few days before you held, is special. I have read and reread your letter many times and I only got it this afternoon. I search for every nuance or hidden meaning. I reread to be sure I got the meaning you were trying to convey. Up until now, I've only had a phone call, your voice. Now, there is something tangible. It helps. I imagine you can understand and that you, too, have read my letters more than once. Also, it evidences trust. Had you been unwilling to write to me at all, ever, I know I could not have continued to write. I would feel like I was talking into a void. Please do not worry about your handwriting; no one has a worse handwriting than I do. My friends ask me not to write unless I have a typewriter. Also, please do not apologize for how you write, what you say, or for your nervousness. We are both nervous right now and shall probably remain that way for a while. Do you cherish any word from me? If you do, if your heart lifts when you see my letter among your morning mail, then certainly you must know I feel the same way. I don't care how well you say it, just say it. Let me hear from you. I want to know. We are not writing for posterity. We are writing for knowledge, knowledge of each other. There is so much to catch up on.

I would never reach out to you to play games, to pretend with one another. It would be a waste of time. That is not how I live or how I relate to people. I have a young friend in Chicago who says, "Jazz, you must wonder why you never get any mail." It is not like I can sit down and write a short note saying, "Hi, how are you? I'm doing well." When I write to you I know you really want to know everything I'm feeling. That's an accurate statement. Robert, you and I have so much to learn about each other. If I start being coy it could take us forever. We don't have forever. I have an innate sense of how brief life is. I do not spend my time talking about the weather.

I do not need Lilly's certification that I am okay. I never did. I believe in therapy. It has made a major difference in my life. I am too impatient to wait and to struggle along on my own, attempting to resolve emotional issues. These people spend about thirteen years studying personality. There are only a few types, and if they can help me solve a problem in half the time it would take me to solve it alone, I'm seeking their help. Therapy does not work for everyone, and I believe there are many bad therapists who screw up people's lives faster than they could screw them up by themselves if left alone. But I knew what I wanted to do and how to find the person who could help me to understand my own destructive behavior, and change took place immediately. I do not believe one has to be sick to go. I believe I was smart to go and yes, you couldn't be more accurate about the pain. Looking at self is always painful; few people have the courage to do it. I did.

Was I proud (since she is a published author and one seeks approval from their peers) when she said my writing would one day be my gift to the world? You bet I was.

I never felt I was not okay. My life is happier now. No, I am not preparing you for any bad tales. Sad, yes. But bad, no. No one, absolutely no one, who has ever read my work has ever felt it was obscene. Those were my internal fears, part of what kept me from publishing, but when you read it I know you, too, will agree; it is not obscene. It is beautiful. Someone said last week "lyrical prose." It is not that my life was so horrible; in many ways it is very typical of what happens to women. Many women have had worse lives. I have the talent to articulate our experience. There is only one major difference about my work. They are comparing me to the French existentialists and Simone de Beauvoir's *The Second Sex*. Her work is enormous and I don't believe you would want to wade through the entire thing, but you might want to get it from the library and check out her section on women as the Subject of desire rather than the Object. I believe it is okay to say I desire rather than just being desired. That is untraditional and makes me more vulnerable.

Robert, part of loving you is knowing I don't have to prove myself to you, knowing you, too, care for me. When I said trust the person you used to know, I said it because regardless of the time lost, I am still that person. I do not treat my fellow man any differently today than I did when I was constantly in church. Have no fear; I will continue to share with you. So much so until you will probably scream for me to lighten up and be less intense. I want a relationship with someone who will struggle together with me, be engaged. Thanks for restating that you see me as special. I want to be special to you.

I smiled when you said you saved my letter for a day. Friends tell me they wait until they can sit quietly at night with a cup of tea, that my letters are like dessert. What praise especially from you, to know you enjoy my letters. Savor me. Words are my gift and there is no one, no one I would rather give that gift to. No, you are not a masochist, enjoy me as I do you.

Yes, of course, I have discussed you with Lilly. She understands I am going back to the beginning of my life, searching for causes for the direction my life took, understanding my mother's part in that. She thinks you sound like a really good person and she is concerned for us. Concerned we will get together at some point, have a physical relationship, and you, because of your goodness will be engulfed in guilt and therefore make me feel guilty. I am her client, so it is me she is worried about. She also has pointed out to me, that although you have been married thirty-two years it does not necessarily mean that emotionally it is a good marriage. She is not saying it is not; she was just pointing out how often a community, or friends, see a marriage as perfect, as I see yours, when in actuality that marriage has been emotionally dead for years. She also pointed out, a statistic I am aware of, that most men never leave their wives. She added as well that she has known of instances such as what has happened to us where the people eventually got together and had a wonderful life together. This is her talking, not me. I will expound later on how I see what is happening to us, my original contact with you, what my intentions were, and how the interaction is affecting me. For now I want to keep answering your questions.

My sister, Jessica, has always known of my feelings for you, but while we were in North Carolina I told her that I had tracked you down, called you, and I had written to you but had not heard back and did not know if I ever would, but that it was okay, I had done what I set out to do. She understands how I feel because our mother also railroaded her first marriage, too, which was an eighteen-year nightmare. Jessica said she could just imagine if her new husband got such a call how he might respond. I told Jessica I understood the guilt you would feel if you responded.

Robert, there are just some things you have to do and then let it go. I am so grateful and so glad you could respond to me, but if you had not been able to I still had to write that first letter. I had no choice. It was the appropriate thing for me to do. I owed you that letter. It was thirty-odd years too late but I owed it to you. Jessica understands and would never pass judgment. I later told her by phone that you had called and we'd had a tearful reunion. She was glad. I also told her you felt like a philanderer just placing the call. We are not in touch often, so she knows of only our first conversation. I don't discuss it with people. I don't think we understand it yet. I could not explain it to someone else. I hope you realize that some of your fears must have to do with you and what you are feeling. Let me reassure you again. You have nothing to fear from me. I will never come to you. If we see each other even in two years it will be when you decide you are ready for that. On paper, I will seduce you in any way possible, and I see no harm in that if that is all we can have. Do I want you? Of course I do. I would love to spend the rest of my life with you, to wake every morning with you by my side. But would I want to be sitting in front of the fire some winter night when we are sixty-five and have you brooding about your relationship with your children because of what you did to their mother, never. I'm not that stupid. I love you, Robert, and part of that loving includes wanting your happiness. I love you but I don't have to have you. That would be the icing on the cake, but right now I have more of you than I ever dreamed possible in this lifetime. For now, that suffices. We don't even know if we would like each other if we had the chance to be together.

You feel so right to me that I find it hard to convince myself of that. We might not be compatible, but who knows. We may just have the perfect relationship as it stands. It does not stop me from desiring you, however. Desiring you like no one I've ever desired in my life. There is some incredible hook to childhood memories and your first love, especially if they happen to be as brilliant as you are. God, I miss you.

Thomas Trout is a multimillionaire. I paid rent when I lived with him. I bought most of the groceries. Not because he required it, but because I believe people with money, especially people with money, need to know you are with them because you want to be and not because of something they might be able to do for you monetarily. I think I am the only woman in his entire life who he felt would be with him even if he did not have a dime. That was a great gift I could give him. I'm glad I could do it. It was not entirely unselfish on my part. I would never place myself in a position of dependence, and that has something to do with my ability to trust.

I say all of this because I hear you questioning my contact and exposure to you. Robert, my original contact was to correct a wrong. I must be honest and tell you that your response to me is greater than I expected or could have ever dreamed or anticipated. Am I pleased? You bet. Surprised? Absolutely. Elated? I'm ecstatic. Confused? A little. Right now, we don't fully understand exactly what we are feeling or where this is going or what might happen. I only know I trust our goodness. We are mature enough and smart enough not to do anything foolish or stupid. We both want the best for each other. For now, I am pleased for the contact. I love, simply love, being able to talk to you. I feel at home, as though I'd never lost you. I'm loving it. Can you? Robert, do you feel joy as well and not just fear and doubt and questions?

Your love empowers me. I do more, am more productive, more effective, happier, as I go through my day because you care about my welfare. I want my love to give you some of those feelings, too, not just fear.

I shall probably talk to you before you get this, but you know me, I want it down in print.

Blessings,

Jasmine

Jasmine Carrietté

June 22, 1987

Dear Rob,

    I promised I would explain "What went wrong?" It seems an overwhelming task and may take a lifetime, but I shall try. Since we grew up together, at least you knew my family and background and that should help in the explanation, but I want to expand on that so you can understand it from my perspective. Those early years are crucial to my story. The overriding issue, which carries implications for every major life decision, was my lack of self-esteem. You get that at home. I will endeavor to explain the deprivation I experienced, but it will not be easy. The explanation will be lengthy, but hopefully, I can convey some sense of the isolation I felt, how that was expressed in my lack of self-confidence and the impact it had on my life. It takes so long to restage the roles our parents set for us. It took me fifty years.

    In my first letter to you I spoke of my fear of being able to prove my virginity. Can you see that had I been more self-confident, I would not have felt so unsure or worried so much about that? You seemed to demand more of me. It went far beyond virginity. You expected more. Unstated and unexpressed was my fear that I could not deliver, not just the virginity, but all or whatever it was that you might expect of me. At a time when every other male was trying to get me to be more physically intimate with them, you were doing quite the opposite, keeping me at a distance. Only one man in those early years of dating ever actually tried to force himself on me. He was unsuccessful, but the fact that he even tried implied to me a question about my character. I was insulted he thought I was that kind of person, a girl who would "do it." However, almost any man I ever dated tried to get more familiar with me than you did. Everyone else made it evident they desired me even though they did nothing overt. I wanted you; but you never got physical, ever. I felt out of control. While I was overwhelmed with feeling, you appeared uninterested. So here I am, not understanding or knowing about your fear that something might happen, or your recent explanation that you probably had a Madonna complex about me. The nearest I can remember, we never discussed sex very much. All I knew was your standards were much higher than those of anyone else. Had I been more secure, I would have known I could meet your standards. I did not. I had never been able to please my parents. I did not think I would ever be able to please you either. Your standards scared me.

It is really strange, Rob. Let me leap forward until just after your recent call to me in North Carolina. After all the pain of the last year of living with Thomas Trout, while I was in therapy with Lilly, and then coming here to Smith and the work I have been doing, after finally coming to terms with what has actually happened in my life, it was all I could do just to understand, cope, and survive. It was not until after your call and after the good years of being nurtured, which I have had here at Smith, that I can finally have the luxury to really feel the grief of what happened to me. The greatest part of that begins in my childhood with the deprivation, which engendered that total lack of self-confidence and self-esteem. For now, this minute, you will just have to take my word for it and bear with me through this long explanation of so many years, before you can either agree or disagree with me that the lack of self-esteem, learned at my mother's knee, is indeed what went wrong.

Certainly, it cannot be argued, my mother influenced my initial and key decision to marry Allen rather than you. Answer me this? What kind of mother would rather see her child married to a man thirteen years her senior who drives a bus for a living, as opposed to an up-and-coming young man her daughter's age, intelligent, confident, educated, and with a secure future? Remember, in those days young women married for security. Can you imagine what distortion she must have provided for herself, to engineer a marriage to the former rather than the latter? Think of your own daughter and how you might feel about her potential husband. Can you see how far from loving my mother's behavior was? Through the years it was evidenced in many more ways than that, both for me and for my sister, but this one very clear-cut example set the pattern that was to follow.

As I have said to you from my initial contact, you were my only hope for recovery from that childhood of deprivation. Why you? Because of your intelligence and because of your love for me. Both of those qualities might have redeemed me. Granted, you would have been fighting a tough battle because I had years of bad input from her to overcome, but I do believe, have always believed, that with your strength, your mind and your love, I would have at least had a fighting chance.

Briefly then, let me sketch for you some of the major incidents of the early years, and then I'll try to give you more detail on the later years so you can see the precipitating incidents which finally brought me to Smith and to you.

I married Allen in December of 1952 and we lived in an apartment across the lake from the Catholic hospital in Baton Rouge. Here is a brief synopsis of our wedding night:

"Are you ready?"

"Ready?" I'd been waiting ever since I could remember, but somehow I thought there would be more of a ritual, some kind of initiation to such an important occasion. We were lying side by side, fully gowned or robed. *Ready?* I was anxious, excited, but surely there was more to it than this. He was untying his robe and climbing on top of me. He pulled my gown up but he never touched me, not once. There was no kissing, no stroking, no holding, no cuddling, nothing. Within minutes it was over. I had been consciously waiting for this night since I was about eleven. I was just nineteen. Surely something had gone terribly wrong. I had read everything I could get my hands on at the library, and even though embarrassed, had risked asking the rather grim librarian for books from the closed shelves. No one would talk to me about it, but I remembered one of my mother's sisters saying the first time felt like somebody trying to put their elbow in your ear. That would have been an improvement. I felt nothing, not even pain. There was a little blood but not much. At first, I thought nothing was going to happen because he didn't seem to be able to get it in, but finally he did, managing even then to never put his hands on me. Nothing, mostly I felt nothing. Surely it would get better. What about the earth moving, butterflies being released, that succession of waves I had read about? Was I so different? Had I malfunctioned? Surely it was me. My husband was thirteen years my senior. Certainly he knew how to do it.

Unbelievable, isn't it? Rob, I cannot tell you the pain I feel about that night. It is greater now in the remembering of it than it ever was then. Then, I could not know. I could not let myself know, for if I had, I could not have survived. I realize you were not as experienced sexually then as you are now, but my darling, I cannot imagine that there would have ever, on any occasion, been an incident even close in similarity to the one I've just described had my new husband been you. My grief for myself as I write this feels heavy. Do I really want to relive this pain? I want you to know me. I feel that you want to know me. I feel that as I have felt it from no other in my life ever.

Five months after marriage I was pregnant. Unplanned but I certainly wanted children. It was just a little sooner than we had expected. Recall, birth control was not as sure in those days. Can you believe condoms are back in vogue? What horrible memories they hold. I hated them then and they hold terrible memories for me of my life with Allen. My daughter was born in February of 1954; my son in July 1955, eighteen months apart. Just before my son was born we bought my family home, and my mother and father built a new, smaller house at the end of the road. I did not work during my children's preschool years. Intellectually, I could never do that again, but I am glad I was home with them during the first six years of their lives.

To keep myself occupied I was at the church every time the doors opened. I ran everything there they would let me run and did community volunteer work as well. I taught books to the Women's Missionary Society, winning state awards for my endeavors. I taught the Girl's Auxiliary, remember those? I was the director of the preschool and nursery department for several years, and then I began teaching the eighteen to twenty-five-year-olds in Sunday school. Most of the young people were in college, and a young man named Daniel Mason became a major influence. He encouraged me to go to college. Allen was on the road most of the time. I was looking for a diversion. I was a voracious reader, bored to death, sexually lost. Reading Oscar Wilde, Sinclair Lewis, and D. H. Lawrence left me with many questions. Daniel was ten years my junior, perfectly acceptable by today's standards but unheard of then. Many nights we sat up and talked for long hours about major life issues. I loved him very much. He was eighteen. I was twenty-eight with two children and an absentee husband. Daniel saw me as a person of value and stimulated me intellectually. He was a brilliant electrical engineer. We were never lovers. That was not something I could have ever considered at the time, but we loved and supported one another. My Sunday school class started off with two young people in it, and when I left the Good Hope Baptist Church there were sixty people in my class. Even then I knew that if there was a God he was nothing like the image we had reduced him to.

We had been married eight years when Allen became impotent. You must understand, not only was I ignorant about sex, we were in a different age. People did not talk about sex. Allen and I used to play cards with the Garritys. Do you remember them? Well anyway, we played cards with them and with Lyle and Jennifer. I was reading everything I could get my hands on, so although not formally educated at that point in my life, I was exposed. I was hungry, desperately searching for answers to how I felt. No one in my circle of friends expressed the yearnings I did. Allen is a good person. A good country boy who has done very well with his life. He is a marvelous father. He could not give emotionally what I needed because he did not understand what that was, but he would have given it if he knew. For a man who decided he was not going to dig his living out of the ground as his father had, he did very well, and rightfully, he should be proud. Although it seems trite to say it, never were two people more wrong for each other. As I have stated earlier, he was perfect for my parents. He was the son they had always wanted and finally I was able to give them that, and they, too, were perfect for him. He was one of seven children and now he was of prime importance to someone, my parents.

Even now twenty-seven odd years later, do you notice how I skip over Allen's impotence and move on to other things? It's easier that way. When you do that in real life the problems/tragedies really back up.

Well, there I was, twenty-eight years old reading *Lady Chatterley's Lover*, etcetera, just beginning to come into my own strong feelings about sexuality, and my husband is impotent while I am dying to discuss, talk about, experiment with, oral sex and everything else possible. Well, to make a long story short, I finally mentioned oral sex. I mentioned it while playing cards one night. I wanted to know if people in real life did such things or if it was only in books, and if my desire for and curiosity about it were perverse. No one answered. But the next day Jennifer (yes, your sister-in-law) called to tell me, "I didn't want to say anything in front of the others, but yes, Lyle and I have oral sex—or at least he has oral sex with me. It's just not something I can bring myself to do for him, although he wants me to, but he seems to enjoy it and I let him."

I find it interesting that the first breakthrough in my wall of sexual silence was provided by one of your family members. Rob, I don't know well the person you have become and I'm not sure if the person you were when I knew you could ever remotely understand such ignorance, but no one in my circle of friends shared sexual information.

For the last three years of my marriage, Allen was impotent. He never had an erection yet he was able to have an orgasm occasionally. We were probably one for the medical journals. Do you think that is possible, impossible? I endeavor to be honest and fair in my judgment even all these years later. I know from our discussions he would agree. He was entirely flaccid. He never disputed that. Therapists I have talked to cannot understand it, but I am here to tell you that with the right, cooperative wife who is willing to position herself correctly where gravity helps, and allows him to use his hands to, yes, "stuff" himself inside her (all the while being careful to never touch her), a man can have an orgasm without an erection. I defy anyone to prove otherwise. I lived it. I try not to kid myself about things. I can recall even now the pain of having almost his entire hand stuffing his penis inside my body and of the many efforts, which proved futile and frustrating for both of us. He refused psychiatric help. Not only would he not see a therapist, he would not even see a medical doctor. Can you know, ridiculous, no of course you cannot, imagine what it is like to have a husband who cannot have an erection. It is not something you can share with your female friends over coffee. Not that there aren't other equally pleasurable means to have an orgasm, but they were not emotionally acceptable to Allen. He could not allow himself to manually stimulate me to orgasm, and cunnilingus was out of the question. My desire for fellatio was not something open for discussion, much less practice.

Of course, I was not sure it was not my fault. Indeed, I believed it was my fault, for if I was pretty enough, attractive enough, was not a freak as my mother had described with my forty-two-inch bust, then he could have gotten it up with me. Crass but true. All of my life my mother had taught me how to dress to disguise my large breasts. I was never allowed to wear sweaters like all the other girls, and I had to always have dresses that were buttoned down the front or some other device to hide the fact there was such a large expanse there. In eleven years of marriage to Allen, he never once put his hand on my breasts. I did not think there was something wrong with him. It confirmed my mother and my sister had been accurate. I was a freak.

In all the years I had known Allen, I never saw him read a book. He was such a good person, but before it was all over I began to feel that if one more person told me how good he was I was going to hit them. There is more to life than being good. What about exciting? Always, from the very beginning, I don't know where I got it, but I've always had an innate sense of how brief life is. I've never made decisions based on what other people think, and I've never made decisions which burdened my children with the understanding of how much I've given up because of them. Hopefully, I've given them a heritage that says it is all right to value self.

Anyway, sex was not what was wrong between Allen and me. It was a symptom of what was wrong. After three years, I could no longer cope with the issue by myself. Finally, I saw a lawyer who advised I approach my parents to see if they would allow me to come back home for a few weeks until I could get a job and get settled somewhere else. Allen and I walked together down to their house. You must understand that our marriage was an example to the community. Everyone thought we were the perfect, happy couple. My parents adored Allen. At the close of the discussion they said no, I could not come home, and they turned to Allen and said, "We don't really understand what is going on, but we want you to know that as long as you live, you have a home here, no matter what happens between you and Jazz." The legal advice I had just gotten could not have been worse, but of course he was advising me, expecting a normal parent-child relationship.

With Allen's approval, I went to a motel alone, my first night away from my children since their birth, to consider the next move. My parents, because we lived next door, across the hollow, could see I was gone for the night. They called the minister.

I must go work. Please suspend your judgment until you have the entire story. I may be asking the impossible. It was great talking to you on Sunday. I cannot believe that for a woman who is afraid of nothing, I turn to jelly at the sound of your voice.

I hope you have a good week. Know you are loved. This is going to be a depressing story. It does get better. It only takes twenty years.

God, I have courage.

Jasmine

Jasmine Carietté

July 25, 1987

Dear Rob,

It is so good to begin to know you again. I really appreciate the long telephone visits. They make me feel so close to you. Thanks for calling. Continuing a part of that conversation, may I explain I have a history of being in situations where men deny me. As my story unfolds you will see that. Only then can you understand my overreaction to what I perceive (probably inaccurately) as your vacillating about when and if you can ever see me. I don't have to see you now. I don't have to know when I'll see you, but if you were to say you could not ever see me, that puts me in a different position. From my perspective I cannot ever again be in a friendship where I'm denied as a person. Soon you will understand why I can't do that. As I said earlier, I'm not talking about sex; I'm talking about seeing. Men never seem to understand I, too, play a part in making a decision about what happens between us. Should I see you, of course I would want to touch you. But would I? No. I love you, Rob. Being sexually involved with me would be devastating to you. That is not what I want for you and it's not what I want for myself. When I thought you said you could not see me ever it made me feel like a leper or something, and I do not want to feel like that. I've already been involved with men who, for some perverted reason of their own, wanted to keep me in the closet. No more.

Let me continue. Glenn Bowman, the minister my mother called the night I stayed at the motel, came to counsel me. He arrived at my motel room quite late that night. I was still fully dressed with only my shoes off and sitting cross-legged in the middle of my bed. He sat across the room in a chair and tried to reason with me.

Glenn said many things that night, but two things especially stuck with me. The first was:

"Jasmine, I believe most people can profit from therapy. Why do you think I would believe I need it and you don't? It's not disparaging for me to say I think you need help. You're in a terrible situation. I'm not putting you down when I say I think you'd benefit from therapy at this point in your life."

Desire Makes the Difference

The other thing he said, which I recall as wise advice, is:

"Go back home. You don't leave when things are bad. You leave when they're good. Go home and finish your education. Go home until Allen is better and able to cope with the fact you're leaving him. You won't be sorry. I know time seems of the essence, and I also know how hard it is to live under the same roof with someone you don't love anymore, but I'm telling you, you won't be sorry you waited. Go back and get help and make your decisions from a place of strength."

Glenn was right on both counts, the fact that I would benefit from therapy, and the fact that I would feel better about leaving when things had improved. Surely you remember the environment of that community enough to understand that had a typical Southern Baptist minister been there at the time, he would have patted me on the head, told me to go home and give it to my husband whenever he wanted it, to have a daily family devotion and ask for God's will to be done. Suffering was some sort of price exacted by their demon god. I recall once being visited in the hospital by one of the good ladies of the church after emergency surgery. As I lay near death she held my hand to pray with me and, before beginning, asked what I had done to cause God to discipline me so and would I repent. I did then and always shall cherish Glenn Bowman for being at the right place at the right time in my life. I love him, truly love him for that.

Not until many years later was I to realize I was an attractive woman sitting in a motel room late at night, alone, with this handsome man, telling him I had not had sex in three years, and not once did he even get out of his chair or come near me. After my divorce, most of my propositions would come from Southern Baptist ministers. I had little understanding then that for many of them the attraction to the ministry was their expectation it would repress and control their sexual appetite.

The next morning I went back to Allen and my home on Tiger Bend Road. I had expected to go back the following morning to start a formal separation and divorce proceeding. Instead, taking Glenn's advice, I told Allen I wanted to see a therapist and he agreed to the expense.

That day I made my first call to a psychiatrist. It was 1962. In those times, among my acquaintances in the South, this was an unprecedented step. Immediately, you were considered insane. I didn't care; I wanted relief from the confusion I felt. Everything I had been raised to believe was being called into question and I didn't have the answers anymore. Finally, Allen agreed to go to therapy with me. He went for only three visits and the psychiatrist said to me, "It would take a year to get him to talk to me. He is pretty happy with his life. He cannot admit he feels any hostility toward you. We could pull his life apart. I am not sure we can put it back together again. I believe he would be despondent if you left him now, but do it gradually, as he can accept it, little by little and he will adjust. Ask for a trial separation and when he can accept that, later, ask for the divorce."

Together we explained to Allen that I was going to continue college, and even though he was paying for it, I might leave him when I got out. He said that was a risk he would take, so I stayed in school and stayed married. The psychiatrist said I did not need psychiatric help, that I simply needed someone objective to talk to. He explained I was feeling the burden of carrying all the problems by myself for three years. He said, "You feel isolated because of the world you are in. There are other worlds." For the first time in years I felt hope. He advised a counselor just to listen for a while. My minister told me Dick Paine, the chaplain at a local hospital, had a degree in psychology from Yale and did counseling at the hospital. This would take me out of my community and the gossip. Glenn made the appointment for me. Dick Paine called the psychiatrist I had been seeing for a referral and an update on my case, and soon I found myself standing just outside Dick's office awaiting his arrival from a Monday morning staff meeting.

He arrived, introduced himself, invited me in and told me to have a seat. Little did I know this would begin an odyssey, which would change the direction of my life. If only there were large hand-painted signs emblazoned in the heavens announcing the arrival of disaster. No such luck; more likely disaster comes prettily packaged. Not necessarily physically, it can be mental. The seduction of brightness, to me, is a palpable aphrodisiac. The mental pyrotechnics—the verbal interchange—are the strongest turn-on ever.

You've got to understand this is hindsight. That day I felt nothing but fear. No matter how badly one wants to change their life, doing it

Desire Makes the Difference

is hard, terrifying. There were major sexual problems in my marriage and I was going to talk to this minister about it. Scary.

I had been in therapy with Dick Paine for three months when he said to me, "Pull your chair around to the side where I can see you. Lay back and rest your head. Close your eyes. Here, let me give you a stool for you to put your feet on. I want you to be totally relaxed and comfortable. Now close your eyes and I want to ask you some questions. We have been stuck now for several weeks, quite unproductive sessions. I want you to go deep now, deep into your subconscious. I want you to tell me everything, everything, things you have never told anyone else. I want to know it all."

We were both quiet for a few minutes. I had always sat across the desk from him. I was uncomfortable in this new position. I felt very vulnerable. He turned his swivel armchair to face me. I was at his side. In earlier sessions he had asked why I always buttoned my blouse all the way to the top, and now he asked me to undo several buttons. None of this could ever happen to me now, not at this age and not with my experience, and I am not sure if you will be able to understand how ignorant and inexperienced I was at this point in my life. It seems impossible when I look back on it that I could have had two children (one constantly ill), several operations, run a household, coped with a stress-filled life all on my own as my husband traveled for a living, and have been so dumb. But I hope also you have read and know something about the transference which takes place in therapy. Dick Paine was like God to me. I would have done anything he said, and did. With the exception of Glenn, Dick was a man in my life who accepted me as I was, unconditionally. Of course, nothing could have been further from the truth, but that was how it appeared to me that day. I hope, if you have a problem understanding this, that you will read *Sexual Intimacy Between Therapists and Patients* by Kenneth S. Pope and Jacqueline C. Bouhoutsos, which will shed some light on a seemingly incomprehensible scenario.

Dick started questioning me about my techniques for masturbating. He then insisted I think of him while I masturbated. I said no; I did not. He insisted I did. It got worse from there. He finally told me he had been counseling me for three months while he sat there with an erection and there was no point in both of us suffering. I was sexually deprived. He was sexually needy. We were to comfort each other.

I am sure you may want more details about this sordid story, but I find it very difficult to continue. For one reason, I am no longer the person this could happen to; for another, I repeated the pattern for so long it is still terribly frightening to me.

I will condense it to what you have here and if it calls for further clarification, ask me. For the next four months I went once a week to Dick Paine's office for "counseling." He stood in the corner of his office, fully clothed, away from the window, and I sucked him off. I use that term because that was literally how it was. He tied a handkerchief around his penis so the zipper would not scratch him and I would not get makeup on his trousers. He never touched me, not ever, not even the hair on my head. I was in love with this man as one is during transference. As an adult, and with the exception of Glenn Bowman, he was the first really bright man I had ever known. We often talked of Faulkner, whom I loved. I did not know another soul I could talk to about Faulkner. They would not have even known who Faulkner was.

I was not allowed to touch him anywhere with my hands because I might wrinkle his suit. The only contact was mouth to penis. I, of course, had never done this before. I had read about it but had no idea how to do it. So calmly, in his quiet, most professional counseling voice, Dick instructed me in how to pleasure him. I, on my knees in front of him, could not respond verbally, my mouth was full. "Pull your lips over your teeth. Don't use your tongue on the glans. The tongue feels like sandpaper and the glans is too sensitive." Many years later I'd discover he was a minority of one about that, but for now he was the experienced one and I was the initiate.

I'll get back to this part of the story, but I want to explain briefly what was going on at home. Allen, in an endeavor to ease his tension over performance, had brought home a bottle of whisky. We had agreed beforehand to try having a drink together first. I was twenty-eight years old and this was the first drop of alcohol to cross my lips. At this stage of questing in my life, I wanted to try everything. Although we lived eighty miles from New Orleans and the famous Bourbon Street, I had never been there, so I asked Allen to take me. I tried three times to learn to smoke, but ended up at the doctor's office all three times, so gave that up. Bradley was very small at the time and he, as children will about new events going on at home, announced to my parents Allen and I had had a cocktail. This, coupled with their new knowledge that I was thinking about divorce, led them to try to have me committed to a mental institution. This seems so out of line and incomprehensible it boggles the mind, but in reality that is what happened. Do you remember, at this very same time, Earl Long's wife had the governor of Louisiana committed? In Louisiana you did not have to have a psychiatrist's signature to have someone committed. All you needed was the signature of a parent or a spouse.

My parents, really my mother with my father acquiescing, went to Allen and said, "If you don't commit her, we will. We don't want to go over your head but we will if we have to." Allen replied, "I don't want Jazz to divorce me, but I won't have her committed to stop her." Allen is a generous, kind man.

I, of course, did not know all of this was going on. After Allen's refusal to cooperate with them, they went to my counselor, Dick Paine, to get his help and support in having me committed. They had discovered they could not do it alone since I was married. Months later, Dick told me that in all of his years of practice he had never seen parents more hostile to a child. He said every time he tried to say something complimentary about me, they immediately rejected it. He explained to them he had spoken to the psychiatrist who had seen me, and that the psychiatrist had said not only did I not need psychiatric help, my problem was that I was extremely intelligent and living in such a limited environment. Dick elaborated that my problems stemmed from my daily encounters with people who saw things from such a closed point of view, which ultimately isolated me. They would hear none of it.

I hate to leave this story at such a crucial point, and again I must ask you to withhold judgment until you have all of the facts. Is that hard for you? Impossible? I hope not. It is just that with the busy routine of living and all that is required each day, plus trying to catch you up a little bit via the telephone on the person I am right now, it seems like I am taking forever to bring you up to date on my past, so I wanted

Jasmine Carrietté

to at least get something in the mail to you. As it is, it has been several weeks since you have heard from me. Rob, this week, after our long conversation last weekend, I have felt so close to you. The connection is enriching my life. It feels so positive.

I am glad, my love, to have you.

Jazz

February 14, 1988

Dear Robert,

Well, my dear man, much has changed in our friendship since last I wrote. I wish I had some clue as to exactly what those changes were. I don't, so pretty much I feel I'm writing in the dark to some phantom. Since you won't talk to me, let me see if I can phrase it so at least you will understand what I am feeling and the mind-set I have gone through since your withdrawal.

The last time we talked on the phone, as far as I can remember everything was fine. Nothing you said indicated to me you were having second thoughts about being in touch with me. You made no mention of any new, renewed feelings of guilt, etcetera. I just sort of went along my merry way. Happy to have you back in my life. Thrilled to share what I could with you. Glad for your support. Happy for your welfare and to know your life had turned out pretty much just the way you wanted it to. Glad for the success of your children and your wife and your business. I cannot tell you how very good it felt to be able to talk to someone from my childhood who remembered and knew the same things and the same people and the same routines and circumstances of growing up that I did. It was wonderful, simply wonderful. I cherished the times you would call and we could talk for an hour on the phone and share, bringing each other up to date on the intervening thirty-five years.

I must say I felt no censure from you. I felt support and love and a real genuine warmth and gladness to have me back in your life. I felt at peace about my decision to finally right an old wrong. I had deeply hurt the person I loved the most and had never been able to tell him I loved him. Finally, after all these years that was not only made right, I had, as well, all of the things I mentioned above, which I never in my wildest dreams expected to have with you.

And then . . . and then, I told you about my past and suddenly, you were gone from my life again. Not by my doing. I had not been the one to leave this time. It was you and I did not know why, but I could guess.

I tried to understand, but it was hard. I felt what happened before was done out of ignorance and the fact I was essentially a child responding to my mother's desires. I hold you responsible now.

We are adults, but then alternating with the moments of anger at your sudden withdrawal of your friendship and support, unannounced and unexplained, I would have moments of realizing I had done it to you years ago. You certainly have the right to do the same.

Then yesterday, out of the blue, I received a birthday card from you. I don't understand, Robert. I was thrilled, of course, to hear from you. I don't know how you even knew it was my birthday. Had I mentioned it at some point? I cannot believe you remember it from all those years ago. I am totally perplexed and so I am simply going to ask you the following.

I beg you to rethink your decision about being able to talk to me at least one last time. I want to remind you of several things:

1) When I originally wrote to you I never ever expected to have an ongoing correspondence with you. I expected to tell you the truth about what happened. Period.
2) When you did call me in North Carolina and we talked, at that point in time I came to expect that, by your response, we would at least send Christmas cards every year and that I would keep you posted when my address changed, but that is all. In other words, we would not be in touch with one another on any routine basis, but we would always know where the other person was.
3) And then you called me back in North Carolina to say you wanted to be sure that I had not misunderstood. You said you would "be in touch *often*." Correct me if I'm wrong, but as I remember those were your exact words. You said you wanted to know everything about me, everything that had happened since you last saw me.

So necessarily, it was at this point in time when I began to change what I expected from our friendship. I know I'm not stupid, so unless I've missed something here (and please do correct me if you disagree with this sequence of events) I have reason to be surprised when suddenly, after over six months, you can no longer speak to me by phone.

Granting you the right to, for lack of any other suitable words, "pay me back" for my cruel treatment of you all those years ago—and please know I do grant you that right with no censure involved (oh, let's be honest, there is a little anger)—let me ask you: If it is not for that reason, then for God's sake what? Are you judging me? If so, why did I not feel it? I felt your sympathy and understanding. Did you change your feelings later?

The only other explanation I can grasp for your losing my phone number, refusing to call, etcetera, is that you are feeling guilty because you are married. Robert, I have a hard time understanding a relationship that closes everyone out of it. I would rather be single for the rest of my life than be married to someone who allowed me no access to having other people in my life. Surely you and Beverly do not live like that. I have said everything I know to say about what I do NOT intend to do sexually with you. Robert, I am not married, but I have a choice in what happens here, too. All of the money and the time and the therapy and the pain would be worthless if now I simply made the switch to married men. I wouldn't do that to myself. Can't you understand that? But I can love you forever and you can be my friend. I need your friendship. Don't you need mine? If you must withdraw your support and your friendship, can't you at least call me one last time and say that to me? Can't you at least say good-bye over the telephone? I'll be moving June 1. Is your choice really going to be one of going back to never knowing where I am in the world again? Is that really how you feel about me? I do not believe I have misjudged you all these years. Please have the personal courage to say good-bye to me. Let's don't script a tragedy by ending this reconnection in this manner. Even good-bye can be said with love and understanding.

I have an incredible new job beginning June 1, and besides all of the other marvelous things about it, it places me in California and Arizona for much of each winter. I thought you would be thrilled to see me next winter, and I was glad you would have a year to prepare yourself for that meeting. Obviously, that is never to be (although it seems childish to me that it can never happen). I can deal with not seeing you, but I can tell you, sir, I am some furious that you deny your friendship to me. Are you that afraid of your own emotions? I have enough strength for us both. Robert, can you really understand what love, real love, is all about? It is not about possession or owning. I love you, Robert; never, never would I do anything ever again to cause you pain. You would not want to live if you were ever physically unfaithful to Beverly. Don't you think I know that about you?

I am writing this letter to say please, please do not do this to us. If you must withdraw, do it in a more caring way. Call me and explain why you must go. Then go if you must, but know I disagree with your decision. Life is so hard. There is too little pleasure and too much pain. Why would someone willingly withdraw from something which nourishes the soul?

I await your response.

Jazz

PS: Regardless of your response, I will eventually send you some pictures I took recently. I am evil enough to want you to see what I think you're missing. Two other thoughts: Did something, God only knows what, happen over Christmas? Could there have been some miscommunication between your mother, Beth, me, and consequently you? I guess I'll never know. Second thought: Would you please read for me *The Denial of Death* by Ernest Becker. Read it twice; it's that deep, you'll need to. It embodies so much of my belief about life. You should have a better sense of my life philosophy.

Robert, I have learned not to be afraid to ask for what I want. Please know I give you the right to refuse.

March 19, 1988

Dear Robert,

This reminds me so much of how I felt in my relationship with you all those years ago, so I understand even better now why I made the decision I did. You make me feel so guilty. Robert, we are worlds apart in our thinking. You are right. We would not have made it together. I am sure I would have left you during the sixties. Without knowing, I feel certain you were in favor of the Vietnam War. We would have divorced over that issue alone, no doubt about it.

Can you know how difficult it is for me to understand your mindset? Your guilt is so enormous. I refuse, absolutely refuse, to accept all of the (excuse me) bullshit that the Southern Baptist Church puts out. From my vantage point, which I admit is limited, you appear to have picked up your life and moved three thousand miles away from Louisiana only to duplicate every manifestation of your childhood and your upbringing, perhaps in an even more rigid way.

Where is the adventure, the risk, the engagement with life, the challenge, the exploration? I am not talking about me. I am not talking about sex. I am talking about fear. You seem so bound with fear of your own emotions.

I can see now that as a woman of intense passion, not just sexually, but about everything in life, the frustration I must have felt at nineteen waiting for you to put your life plan into action. I guess without ever knowing it I saved us both a much more intense pain, for I do believe we sincerely love one another but our personalities are so different. You would not have ever been happy with me. I didn't do anything by the book and I never took anyone's word for anything. I wanted to experience all of life and I have no regrets about my search for self.

Oh Robert, I am so sorry, so truly sorry to have inserted myself into your life again. My preference is just to go away. I promised I would never do that again, so unless you agree to that, I will not. I keep my word. But what I see is going to happen is, simply by abdication, that is the direction we are moving in. You seem unwilling to admit it or verbalize it, however. On your last call it was clear you did not want me to even ask about your family. You felt you were betraying them by talking to me about them. Then what are we to discuss if not your life and mine? You make me feel like a slut, illegal. I'm not, not even close.

About the closet. I never asked to or wanted to be in the closet, so of course you have my permission to tell Beverly about me. The amazing point is that you said to me, "I have to tell her you called." That is not the part you are feeling guilty about. That will not solve your guilt. You never once said, "I must tell her I returned your call." And that is what you are feeling guilty about. Not that I believe you should tell her you returned my call or that you should feel guilty about it.

Of course, I would not wish for you to show Beverly my first letter to you. I believe that concerns only the two of us and it does set straight what I wanted to explain to you. There is one other short letter I recall where I shared my own fantasies about a physical union with you. I would not want you to share that with her. I do believe we both went through a couple of months of fantasy after talking to each other after all these years, but after that, once we settled down, I think we were simply sharing a friendship with a person from our childhood who had been important to us.

I will not tell you when I am in California. I would never put you through that. I will always let you know where I am when I move. I will keep in touch but more like on a yearly basis. I cannot pour out my heart to you, tell you everything about myself and have you unable to share anything of yourself with me. I think you know from my history why I cannot do that. Again, please read Ernest Becker's *The Denial of Death* if you want to understand me and yourself better. If it engenders a desire for further reading, I can recommend some of Kierkegaard and Nietzsche to you.

My God, what a mess. I never intended any of this pain, or discomfort, or guilt. Please tell Beverly anything you like which will make you feel better. Please understand I do not believe any sin has been committed. Please be sure you are not just telling her to relieve your own guilt, far better you should work on why you feel such guilt. Please understand the difference in saying I called or you returned my call. (Again I do not, DO NOT, believe you should tell her you returned my call because that is purposefully, necessarily hurtful, but do be aware that is why you are feeling guilty, over some fantasy, not reality, because nothing has happened.) There is no ostensible reason why we should not all be able to be friends, but that is out of the question because of what you think and feel about me in your mind. I think it is funny that for all of man's effort to control his life, ultimately, it is the mind that deceives us. I'm sorry, Robert. Tell her what you will. I will not bother you anymore. I will send you my forwarding address when I move. I promised you that.

This has been a hard letter. Painful and difficult for you to read, I am sure. Know it grieves me, too. I feel you have such a good mind. I think it a shame you never let it be led by your heart or trusted yourself that you are a good, not an evil, man.

Regardless of our differences in life philosophy, I will always love you. I do feel loved by you. I did as a child and I still do today.

Jasmine

PS: Rereading this letter, I know it will make you terribly angry. You will say, "I know I am a good man, that is why I feel guilty." Trust me, there is more to it than that. Do read *The Denial of Death* and we will talk more about all this in another ten years.

INTERLUDE

Glenn Bowman

Glenn was six foot three with generous black hair parted on the left, beautiful blue eyes, a deep dimple on the right side of his mouth, and a cleft in his chin. Always impeccably dressed, his clothes were expensive, none more so than the understated elegant tie and the handkerchief in his suit pocket folded in the latest fashion. Only twice did I see him in casual clothes. His hairy chest and arms aroused me, so I was grateful he kept them covered.

Glenn talked and walked and moved with a smooth grace. Appearance mattered to him, most of all. He wished that it didn't and struggled with the fact that it did all of his life. He never won that battle even though he saw its falseness, preached against it and wrote about it. It was his personal demon, and the more he reviled it, the greater he struggled to achieve it, this perfect, elusive, wealthy, seductive image that would grab for him, pull back time, and restore to him his lost childhood. When he was young, to survive in Dallas, an appearance of wealth was the one thing he needed and did not have. In this milieu of wealth and power, looks and money and the impact they made were bartered to measure success, and thus he continued the struggle to gain what he had never had, failing to relax and realize he finally had it. The look, the impression he endeavored to convey had somehow arrived. It came late for him, too late.

He was a gorgeous man, newly capped teeth, regal. Women in his congregation swooned over him as they did over most preachers, but more so for him because of his good looks. Fantasy came easily; for an hour every Sunday morning some unpleasant husband was displaced by this figure of movie star quality. At my home there was a man who did not talk. Glenn Bowman was eloquent. He had been the star of the debating team in college and was persuasive. I wanted to be persuaded.

Glenn had an acerbic wit, which could devastate with one word. Most of the women from our church left his presence crushed by his abrupt rejection. I've seen him answer the door at the church parsonage, and holding it only slightly ajar excuse the caller after being engaged in a moment's conversation by thanking her for stopping by. Being dismissed without ever being allowed in, few people called a second time. He was a loner. Scared of people, or disliking those in his congregation, he could not let them in, into his house or his life. He spent most of his days in town at the university or browsing rare bookshops and in the latest art movies. Little time was given to "the flock," so it was no surprise when he didn't last long at this small country church. They felt only hellfire and damnation sermons would keep people on the straight and narrow. They wanted to hear about the blood and the cross. Glenn didn't preach like that. He spoke of himself as their "current" pastor and no one got the joke but me. He said he would not be driven away as the former pastor had been. He wasn't. He left the ministry altogether, but while he was there he changed my life forever.

He had the largest library I'd ever seen, and I hungered for resource books. I had so many questions. I had so wanted an education rather than marriage and was a voracious reader. He came into my life at such a crucial time—1960. I'm glad he was around.

September 12, 1975

Dearest Glenn,

How do I feel about oral sex? How do I feel about oral sex?

> Strongly enough to divorce one man rather than die without experiencing it.
>
> Strongly enough so that, when you posed the question, the nerve endings in my fingertips felt inflamed and touch became painful.
>
> So strongly I sensed a flush as though an electric impulse were racing through my body. Strong enough that I became incoherent.
>
> Strongly enough to feel stalled in an oral stage of development; thus, things of delight are referred to as delicious—hungry for your voice, etcetera.

How do I feel about oral sex?

> That it is one of the most lovely ways to give or receive pleasure.
>
> So strong, an image of you spread supine on my bed with my face nestled between your legs seems to have been with me forever.
>
> So strongly I can almost feel your phallus in my mouth and loving it move down to caress your testicles with my tongue and feel their weight in my mouth.
>
> So strongly it has driven me nearly to the point of insanity, and I long for the sweet pleasure of swallowing your semen and smelling it faintly on my breath and through the pores of my

skin the following day at work, and thus remember the pleasure and joy of you with the image the odor stirs.

So strongly I want to explore every part of your body with my hands and my tongue. I want you to instruct me as I touch you and reassure me that what I am doing is pleasurable to you. I want you to teach me what you like and I want you to talk to me and tell me if it is wrong. I may not be the best technician, but I do have a very real desire to bring you pleasure and joy, because the joy and delight of feeling you in my mouth would be beyond description.

I want to be full of you. I ache with the pain of remembering you and I want to ache with the reality of your phallus in my throat.

My love,

Jasmine

Desire Makes the Difference

By the time I wrote that letter to Glenn—answering his question about how I felt about oral sex—I knew my marriage to Charles was over. I had spent two and a half years trying to save it, unwilling to recognize the impossibility of it. The first year I had spent crying in the office of an expensive psychiatrist in Brookline, Massachusetts. Crying. That is all that I did. I never cried much after that, in part because I never felt so helpless ever again. The problems of the first marriage I could blame on my youth, nineteen, and my parents who encouraged it. This second marriage I erred completely on my own when I should have known better.

Glenn had advised me against it. He stood in my driveway and said, "I would never make such an important decision while I was tied to someone's body." I didn't, or at least I thought I didn't. Charles proposed within two weeks and I accepted. I had a date with Glenn the evening Charles left Baton Rouge. Years later, Charles told me that his proposal came so quickly because he knew that by the time he came back to get me I would be with Glenn. I wished I had believed that someone with Glenn's brains could have found me attractive and interesting.

Little did I know when I wrote that letter to Glenn that it would be thirty years before we consummated our longing to touch one another. I did not understand, yet, and would not for years, that I was far more attractive on paper than in real life. Or that was my guess. When I wrote that letter I had yet to experience the things I wrote of. My first husband, Allen, never had an erection again after I asked about fellatio—at least not with me. Ignorance and naiveté were part of my heritage in the South in the fifties.

For the last two and a half years of my marriage to Charles I had known heartache, trauma, life-threatening situations. Glenn symbolized freedom and play and intellectual companionship. He had saved me years earlier as my pastor, and here he was again on his white horse.

As it turned out, Glenn and I would write to one another for fifty-four-plus years. It still continues, but we would make love only once and see one another on only three other occasions, twice for lunch and once for breakfast, when I was in Baton Rouge to visit my family, with Glenn driving from Texas to meet me. But that would come very late in our lives, far after I realized he could not offer me the intimacy I eventually felt willing to risk, and far after the lust for one another had cooled. My love for him never stopped. Without Glenn Bowman at the small country Baptist church when I first began to think for myself, my life would have taken a monumentally divergent path. For me, he would always hold a special place. But early on, I had desired him—fiercely.

At forty-three, I was pregnant again, and by this time I knew my marriage to Charles was over. I had thought a second divorce would be easier, if it ever came to that. I was wrong. Charles and I had been so in love. We regretted we had found one another so late in life, both thirty-two. How naïve. So at forty-three I was facing starting over again, by myself, a lifetime alone. By the time this relationship was over, I certainly never believed anyone else would ever want me, to be with me, to share with me, to make love to/with me. Charles totally convinced me I was worthless. Years of listening to him berate me had robbed me of any self-confidence. It would be twenty years before talk of verbal abuse by spouses. I recall, especially, a vehement comment one day when he said, "You are nothing but a piece of shit, have never been anything but a piece of shit, and never will be anything but a piece of shit." He, meanwhile, was dating a woman who had green teeth from lack of dental care, and was married to a man who was bisexual and included his male lover in her marriage. I did not understand at the time that this indicated some sense of inferiority on Charles's part. I thought it was me. Isn't that what women tend to do?

We were on a picnic by a river in Vermont, with our friends Marsha and Floyd. We had eaten on the huge flat boulders at the water's edge and were now in for a swim. Charles watched me as I floated far out into the deep swimming hole. Later he would say to me, "You know, you really should not ever float. Your tits are ostentatious." Charles was a biology professor. He never used the word "tits." I had been attracted to his genteel manners. He also knew, as in most marriages one does, the surest way to hurt me. In long talks when we were in love, that early part when you share all of your secrets, I had told him how my mother had spent my years of puberty and breast development (even before the era of added hormones to our food) when my breasts continued to get bigger. She made sure I knew how to minimize their appearance of size with clothing tricks.

Even though saddle oxfords, bobby socks, skirts and sweaters were the fashion by my high school years, I was instructed not to ever wear a sweater because it made me look larger. My sister explained to me that I had no separation in my breasts (I do), that my entire chest was one big breast. I learned at an impressionable age that my breasts somehow made me a freak. When, at twenty-eight, I arrived in college for the first time and was instructed to write a biography of my life, the title was "Size 42 DD." My breasts had come to define me and who I was. I would be fifty before I knew otherwise, for sure.

I knew with a certainty, more than anything else in my life, that I was not prepared to raise another child. This was 1976; abortion was a new option for women. I was also prepared to have the child and give the child to Charles before I left him. But either way, I knew I would leave and would not raise this child. It had taken me almost three years to come to the decision about Charles, but moments to decide on child rearing. When I gave Charles the option, he said, "Bradley (my son with my first husband Allen) has been the light of my life. A child of my own could not be any better."

I had an abortion. The physician wrote "situational anxiety" in the medical records so the insurance company would pay for it. It was an accurate diagnosis. I have never felt I made the wrong decision. Charles was having coffee with his girlfriend while I was having the abortion. I could not leave until he picked me up. He was late—as usual.

Charles and I sat in our living room the night of December 8, 1976, when he quietly remarked, "Tonight, I am either going to kill myself or kill you."

He had a gun that he carried into remote woods while collecting specimens or trapping birds. We had struggled once over that gun as he held it to his head in front of the large bathroom mirror. Unable to take it away from him, I had swept all my cosmetics off the countertop. As glass bottles smashed against the tile like gunshots and I screamed, "Why don't you blow your brains out in front of your mistress?" he dropped the gun.

The next day I took the gun apart, putting one piece in the storage area above the garage and hiding another in the attic.

Charles had no legal permit for the gun, and I was unwilling to drive it to the police station, knowing I would automatically be put in jail for carrying an unlicensed gun in the state of Massachusetts.

My therapist at the time, and the police department, and the judge I eventually spoke with, all tried to tell me that Charles was going to kill me. The police officer said, "You think people do not get killed in Concord. They do. You think the neighborhood protects you. It does not. It is people you know who kill you." The psychiatrist said, "When people talk about suicide what they are saying is 'I place no value on life.' What usually happens is they first kill you and then botch their own suicide, if, indeed, they attempt it at all."

For over two years I had turned into my driveway each night with a constricted dread around my heart, not knowing if I would find Charles hanging from a cellar rafter or in the attic, dead. He consistently refused therapy. Once, I came home and found him cowered in the back corner of my closet, behind my clothes, scrunched down, crying, mumbling, "I can't find my way out." How symbolic is that? Yet, in those days, it was not the first thought entering my mind. Charles was homophobic yet engaged in a three-way relationship that included two men. "In the closet." I totally missed that. Many men and women were attracted to Charles. He was very handsome with a beautiful round ass.

A man being unfaithful to my body would never cause me to leave him, especially if it was atypical behavior and he still loved me, as Charles professed he did. I did not believe there was anything so terrible that we could not discuss it and work it out if we wanted to, both of us working on it for the good of the marriage. I would have never left Charles because he'd had an affair.

What I came to hate him for was his unwillingness to accept and deal with his own guilt, and for transferring and rationalizing his reasons for seeking comfort outside the marriage on me. "Deal with your own shit" became my motto. But it would take fifty years and another long relationship before I would understand people who, although unwilling to cope with all the emotional waste by-products of their own lives, looked for and readily found a repository for placing it on those willing to accept it. It was a transformative experience, and I grieved that it took me so long to arrive at this place of peace.

In the bedroom, I could hold my own. Because no one enjoyed sex more than I did, I never felt threatened about competition in the bedroom, my friend Glenn telling me for years, "Desire makes the difference." Someone Glenn knew had once told him, "I have been to bed with some of the most beautiful women in the world who were as cold as ice—desire makes the difference." I certainly felt desire. It was the cruelty of not taking responsibility for your own emotional baggage, garbage, and dumping it on someone else—in this case, *me*—which I viewed as cowardly and despicable. Own it.

And when I lost respect, I could no longer love Charles.

Love, for me, has always meant, "Do we meet one another's needs?" And for nine years Charles and I did. He wanted a mother and I needed to mother. When I changed and wanted a partner, he was not there. I had made another terrible error in judgment.

Jasmine Carrietté

December 21, 1975

Dearest Glenn,

    My house overlooks a pond in the back. There is a picture window in the kitchen where I sit on a stool and watch the scene below. It is a tranquil picture, which gives me sustenance and strength. It's where I go to replenish my spirit. In the mornings, I sit there with my coffee. There are three bird feeders, a screech owl house high on a pine tree, chipmunks in summer, squirrels always, a mink every spring searching for wood frogs, wood ducks checking out the nesting box and going through their courtship ritual on the water, raccoons eating blueberries in late summer and—each season, no matter what turmoil is manifesting itself in my life—flocks of grosbeaks return from Canada on time each winter, and the goldfinches shed their gray feathers for a brilliant golden dress of summer. It's good to be a part of it all and know that peace remains, if sought. It is the stability in my life. The knowing that there are other, tranquil worlds. I'm striving for that peace and growth in my own life. It helps, meanwhile, to see it acted out below me daily. There are such interesting things going on down there.

    Jasmine

Michael Smith

Michael Smith was the funniest man I ever dated. Whenever we fought he would always stalk off at least three times and then come back, furious, before he actually left. He amused me. He was so predictable about leaving, but what he might say as he left was never predictable. I can hear him now, his footsteps strident . . . across the back deck and down the stairs, the heavy door of his car (always American-made) slamming in frustration. He would come back once to say something relevant to our current argument, return to his car, come back again to say something personally hurtful, and then begin to leave once more, only to come back indoors and tell me for the umpteenth time, "And you took everything Charles had." Charles being one of my ex-husbands whom Michael happened to like. I knew that once he said "And you took everything Charles had" he would really be gone. It was always his parting shot. I could then hear his tires screeching down the curved drive, backing out faster than he drove in.

On this particular day our argument was about sex. We had broken up several months before, but Michael thought our friendship should encompass an occasional lay for him, if he was in need. I had explained many times that I did not work that way. Our relationship was over, although we were still friends, and friendship did not entitle him to the comfort of my bed. Sympathy fucks did not turn me on, and, in this case, I did not believe they would do anything especially constructive for him either. But Michael would whine incessantly because he knew that, more often than not, he could wear me down and win me over. He wasn't winning this battle. As he marched back into the house for the second time, he yelled, "I didn't want to have sex with you anyway—you are a little bit well used."

I couldn't stop laughing. He was absolutely right; I was a little bit well used. But I thought his recognition of that fact and having the balls to say it to my face at this tense moment took a lot of courage. It was the funniest, most right-on thing anyone ever had the nerve to say to me, but the truth hit so close to home I wouldn't be likely to repeat this choice story. What a terrible thing to have someone say about you. As I looked back on the recent years of my life, I could find little to disagree with him about. I'm not proud of that statement, but still, even today, it makes me laugh. Michael had a way of getting right to the point of the matter. He did not pretty things up or waltz around the truth.

Earlier, for three years, Michael and Gerald had been roommates of mine. They were from upstate New York, and I owned a large home in Concord, Massachusetts. They had come to Boston for work. It was during the gas shortage of the early seventies. My job required a lot of travel trying to keep and pay for a home I seldom got to see. Recently divorced, heating this large, old, high-maintenance house was costly, so I took in roommates.

Michael was a young, cold blue-black African-American. He weighed 130 pounds, had a stomach that rippled before abs were popular, and was quite handsome (as were all of his brothers), street smart and witty beyond belief. He made me laugh, and any man who can do that has immediate entrance to my heart. Michael and I had once done lots of things together. We went camping in the White Mountains of New Hampshire. He would fish, and I would swim and hike. We would often go out to dinner together. Certainly we were an odd pair: me, a Caucasian forty-four-year-old female and he, a twenty-four-year-old black male. On one occasion he rushed me to the emergency room in Concord where the attendant, flustered, asked if he was my son. I can't repeat Michael's response.

He never failed to see the humor in racial situations. I asked him once why he never went to the predominately black nightclubs in Boston on the weekends with his friend Gerald. He said, "Those people scare me." One night Gerald found Michael in the men's room at a nightclub, backed into a corner with his arms up over his face. As Gerald approached to ask why he was not out on the dance floor, Michael pleaded, "Get me out of here. These people are crazy."

Michael is dead now, dead at forty-two from drugs and alcohol. He was smart—not well educated—but truly smart. He never had a chance. Environment, expectations, and family history all convened, and he followed his script, exactly.

I can still hear him now as I drove my BMW 2002tii down an exit ramp, saying, "Ride that clutch, Jazz, ride that clutch" with the emphasis on *ride*.

He made fun of me. Not many people do. I appear much tougher than I am, but he saw through the tough to the tender and never stopped trying to get over or relate, even though I really was "a little bit well used."

Michael died, after being in a coma for months. But I still remember him and smile. He deserved more, much more. He was a gentle spirit with a wry view of life and not nearly enough coping skills to support his clear vision. I loved his good spirit.

"Do it, Jazz. Go for it. You must be crazy to quit that job."
"Oh shut up, Michael."
Drawling, "Miz hi an mity."
"I'm not asking for your help."
"Sho nuff. Soon will be. Took everything Charles had; be lookin' for mine next. Insatiable woman; devour men. Po' ole Malcolm never knew what hit 'im. Ought to talk to me. I'd set 'im straight. Watched you in action." (He was referring to the conversation I had with my boss when I told him I was leaving the company.)
"Michael, you sound ignorant. You have no idea, no concept, of what I've faced in this job."
"I know you liked it."
"Liking it's not enough. That's how they take advantage of you, let you do their work. You love it and they take the compensation for it. No more. I'd rather starve first."

"You jes mite get th' chance. 'Course, few pounds wouldn't hurt none."

"Michael, when you come home from work depressed I try to support you about what went on there. Why can't you do the same?"

"I don't quit. I'm tryin' to help. I think you're makin' a big mistake and I'm tellin' you so in time to stop it, but you won't listen. You don't listen to anybody, ever. Smart bitch, think you know it all."

"And usually do."

"See. There's no hope for you."

"You may be right. I'm stubborn, but I'll tell you what—I'll either change the system or die trying. I refuse, absolutely refuse, to use my intelligence for a system that will not compensate me for it. I'd rather fail on my own than succeed for somebody else."

"This the only world we got, Jazz. What you gonna do?"

"I'm going into business for myself."

"Doin' what?"

"I'm not sure yet, but something."

Moving across the kitchen, "Right on, big time lady. Least you starve quicker this way. You can lose money fast in business. Git your agony over with. Jes 'member, Jazz, what goes aroun' comes aroun'. You never be too careful 'bout hurtin' men long the way. Don't 'spect too much support."

"Thanks for your vote of confidence."

"I'm goin' to get the mail. Maybe you won the sweepstakes."

"I'm going to need it, but you can't win unless you play."

I slumped before the picture window in my kitchen, hunched over on the high stool, and watched the purple finches on the feeder at the window. A flock of grosbeaks fought for space at the feeder out in the yard. Charles had placed several tree stumps of varying heights as an approach to the feeder so I could use them as a ladder when I needed to fill it. This was one of those unusually warm days that promised spring would soon be here, and I could catch glimpses of the mink venturing out on the thin ice of the pond in hopes of finding an adventurous wood frog that decided to peep out early.

Banging the front door as he returned from the mailbox, Michael yelled, "You got a letter from your sister, Jessica."

Desire Makes the Difference

"Yeah?"

He handed it to me. "I'm gonna run by the office to see what kinda action they gettin' today. See you later."

"Thanks, Michael. Have a good day."

I poured myself another cup of coffee and went back to the window before opening Jessica's letter.

Jasmine Carrietté

My dear little sister Jazzie,

I'm sitting in my driveway eating a pan of cornbread and drinking coffee with my shorts on. I must cut grass in another week, but it has been a hard winter with several freezes.

How are you? Will the painful times ever end? Where are you with Thomas Trout? He loves you, Jazz, remember that. He may not express it in ways you need for him to, but all along I have told you he loves you, and someday you'll know I am right. He, too, is in pain, and it hurts to watch the two of you in love and unable to reach one another. I don't know how it will all end but I do know he loves you. He always has.

And the job, what about the job? I know you've made a decision to leave, regardless, but are you absolutely certain that is the right decision? So many times in the past, you have been wrong. You have been happy at MultiTech. You make a good income there. Oh, maybe not what you should be getting paid for what you are doing, but an adequate income nonetheless. Do you really have to go? It is the first real security you've had since being single. They offer you good benefits and that is important in your single status. Do you remember how long it took you to find interesting work, which interested you? Can't you find something else before you leave? I feel like a voice in the wilderness shouting 'hark, hark' while you've already gone off to your next decision and left me in the dust.

Look back, Jazz, at how often you've made decisions and then, after the fact, discussed them with your therapist. I'm just suggesting you think before you act. I've put up with nightmare situations in my office because I had no other choice. You know whatever you decide, I'm with you.

Do you need any money? I've got loads. I squirrel it away for rainy days and could send you some if you need it. You know I've thought you should be self-employed years ago. Anyone who always wants to do everything their way as you do should never be working for someone else. You are my bright, brainy, beautiful sister. I hope someday soon, you find your niche.

I love you and miss you and wish you could come for coffee. Can't you move back South?
Love,

Jessica

"What about if I give you a corner office, all glass?"
"Malcolm, that's not it; my office is perfectly comfortable."
"Would an oriental rug help?"
Laughing, "Not at all."
He swiveled his chair to face me, his back ramrod straight. "We've been a good team."
"We have been that." I remembered my first meeting with Malcolm. We had spent over an hour together, each sitting on the opposite ends of the sofa in his pleasant office, but I could get no sense of the man, who he really was.

The personnel office had called to ask if I would take the job if it were offered to me. "I wouldn't take it but I wouldn't turn it down." I pushed as strongly as possible to get some honest dialog going with the man. I was unable to do that. "Why don't we try another interview?" I asked. Before it was over I had requested four interviews with various members of the department in my endeavor to get some sense of who Malcolm was and his management philosophy.

"I will be one out of many employees to MultiTech," I said. "It is far more important that I like you. You are one out of one to me and I will be spending most of my waking time on the job. I need to like this company. How you feel about me is less important; I'm one out of sixteen-thousand employees to you. The job interview is the only time I'm in the driver's seat. I can call the shots, ask all the questions. I believe in laying it all out and not saving any surprises for later. I want you to get to know me as I really am, warts and all, for sooner or later you're bound to see them and best you be prepared for the reality. I've found it saves regrets later. Once I'm employed, it's too late. The interview is fact finding time."

Ultimately, I took the job, fully realizing many of Malcolm's limitations, but I knew, too, that his reserve was not due to self-confidence but rather to insecurity.

As I began to feel my way clear in the new position, I could not believe such a shy man could be the head of the public relations department of this enormous company. Indeed, if he could avoid it, he didn't even want to take a phone call from a security analyst. I became the front man. The legal department called me "the cheerleader" and I really was. Press releases became events with me, and Malcolm was left to his office with his numbers. Before I came, no one in the corporate office even wanted to ask for an annual report. With me, it became a true service department and I put together whatever information people needed. I had all the facts on all the divisions, and Steve Robinson, a Harvard graduate, was one of the best technical writers I had ever seen.

Malcolm provided a quiet stability during days when my personal life was hectic. I came to work to feel in control and peaceful. I made no apology for liking power. I felt as long as somebody had to have it, it might as well be me, and Malcolm abdicated to my strength and my energy. I liked working with all men. I liked being one of only three people in the company who knew there would be a stock split the following day. I dealt with large sums of money and powerful players and I thrived on it. It wasn't my money but it was fun to manipulate it. If trading was stopped on MultiTech stock for any reason, I was the only person in the company allowed to speak to the wire services because I was not a corporate officer. I held them at bay with the gentleness of my Southern charm and the wit of my survival instinct. I could convince people of almost anything, and every year I secured for the chairman of the board, the president, and chief financial officer the time and hearing of seventy of the most prestigious, select group of security analysts in the world.

Malcolm thought it was my sales ability, but Steve watched as I greeted them at the airport, and he believed they came to see me in that white knit dress and be kissed and hugged as I put them in limousines for their ride to headquarters, who knows. Regardless, we had been a fine team; me with my exuberant, outgoing, volatile attitude; and Malcolm with his reticence and quiet, stable ways. But now I was leaving.

Thomas Trout—The Man

The trio rose to sing, and if you had been listening you'd have heard the intake of my breath. Sam and his wife, Jenny, were singing this morning with a man named Tom. I didn't know his name that morning but knew I wanted to. There was a visceral reaction on my part. He was striking. Tall, nearly slouching, but not just relaxed and comfortable, he was casually dressed, one hand tucked inside the back of his belt, palm out. I was too far away that morning to see the freckles across his nose, which gave him an air of innocence he didn't possess, full lips, brown eyes, the same dimple and cleft in his chin as Glenn; all of this framed with an enormous afro, the style of the times. He sang and I was lost. He had the deepest, most beautiful bass voice I had ever heard. I used to sing with my father and was a sucker for deep voices. They made me want to melt. And I felt like I was, that morning, melting. I tried to remember I was in church. He had a mischievous little-boy smile that went with the freckles but not with the body. Every black friend I had was fifteen years older than they looked, so I figured he was about my age, although he appeared much younger. I never expected to get to know him, but that night, when I attended the folk-singing group I had registered for earlier, there he was.

He was a tease and everything he said carried some sexual innuendo or double entendre. I had just turned forty-three, and for the first time in my life I thought I might finally be ready for some sexual freedom and wondered that night if this might be the man I could explore it with.

I was unaware then of the impact a newly single female carried in the imagination of the men in this room. Four of them started courting me that night, Tom among them.

A friend I had known from work for a long time introduced us. We sat on the floor to sing, Tom sitting on my left. When Tom started singing, I wanted to lie on the floor and spread my legs. The man's voice made me weak. I controlled myself and began singing instead with a voice that had not sung in fifteen years and, indeed, had had little reason in recent years to want to. The singing was wonderful fun. It was good to know that I remembered the words to so many folk songs, and that Tom and I both knew the words to all the gospel music.

Through the night, his hand moved from just touching my knee to leaning back, palms down, with his hand brushing my ass and me in no mood for teasing. I wanted to lay him on the church floor and rape him. I turned and whispered in his ear, "If you don't get your goddamn hands off me I'm going to scream." He withdrew his hand immediately and apologized profusely, saying, "I am so sorry; I didn't mean to offend you."

"You're not offending me," I replied. "But I've been celibate for the last six months, and unless you want me to lay you here and now, keep your hands to yourself."

He laughed.

That was the beginning of a lifelong relationship, which would bring me more pain and more joy than any I'd ever known.

Desire Makes the Difference

May 19, 1976
For Thomas Trout

Renewal

I touch your skin of velvet and silk and sensual thoughts invade my brain, uninvited.

You arouse in me—desire.

Long undisturbed, enmeshed in other feelings that lay buried, until you came and kissed them into being like a sleeping beauty, awakened, after years of quiet repose.

How I love the new feeling of aliveness—intense and swelling feelings which overwhelm and inundate me—with you.

Jasmine Carrietté

November 21, 1976

Dear Thomas,

    I love you because
    you allow me to be angry
    you understand my need to be gentle
    you let me touch
    you taught me to play
    you know about fishing
        and crawdads
        and grits
        and catfish
        and gospel singing
        and biscuits and cornbread
        and black-eyed peas
        and hushpuppies
        and trotlines
        and seining for minnows
I love you because
    you give me freedom
    you bring me songs
    you make me joyful
    you arouse desire
    you make me feel young
        and gay
        and carefree
        and lighthearted
        and happy
        and delirious
        and superlative
        and ecstatic
        and beautiful
        and wanted
        and desired

But sometimes I hate you
>	for being cruel
>>		and not doing what I ask
>>		and not seeing me often enough
>>		and never listening when I talk
>>		and ignoring me
>>		and not paying attention
>>		and never saying you think I am pretty
>>		and valuing other women enough to sit by them
>	but not me
>>		and never being dependable
>>>			or reliable
>>>			or trustworthy
>>>			or keeping your word
>>>			or remembering promises

And once I even hated you so much I said I would never go to bed with you again if you were Jesus H. Christ. Fortunately, I realized what a rash remark that was because I simply love your thirteen-inch penis
>	and enormous testicles
>	and beautiful ass
>	and gorgeous thighs
>	and the way you let me play with you for hours
>	and lie between your legs

I love the fact that you are so articulate in bed. You always let me know what you like, or want, or need. Good lovemaking requires good communication and you provide that for me. Besides being very verbal, which lets me know when you feel pleasure,

I love the way you place your hands lightly on either side of my head to guide my movements and indicate what your desires are when necessary. I can feel now the soft touch on my shoulder telling me to back off for a minute because things are too intense unless I wish to rush and give up some of my own pleasure.

I love knowing you are comfortable and unthreatened if unerect, knowing if you are not erect, it is unimportant to me.

I love your maturity to know if you choose to withhold your own orgasm, I do not feel less a woman or responsible; but I also love the security I feel that you know if you want to reach orgasm, I am there for you—you can take your time, you need not rush but rather enjoy your own pleasure, knowing it extends mine and that I will be there for you as long as you need or want me, just as I know you are always there for me until I am completely satiated, spent and exhausted, in that free-floating, relaxed, cloudlike atmosphere of being wrapped in a delicate haze—supported in space—after it is all over.

I love the way you know I want multiple orgasms and you see that my needs are met until I am totally satisfied and screaming for no more pleasure please.

I love the way you move.

I love the thrust of your body and the fact that you never hurt me but hold me so tightly and plunge so deeply inside of me until I scream with the pleasure of you.

I love the way you will not let me go even when I think I have had enough but you know full well I have not; and, you are always right and I am grateful for your knowledge and the additional height of pleasure to which you push me, and the extra satiation of still other orgasms.

I love the way you never say no to me. Can you know what freedom that gives me?

I love the unbelievable sensation of your penis at the back of my throat and being so relaxed with you. I trust so implicitly your tenderness at that time, yet your complete understanding and cooperation to apply just the exact amount of pressure necessary,

but to let me be free to gauge when and how deep. To feel you in my throat is like no other sensation I have ever felt. The trust implied on both our parts says something very beautiful about our faith in each other. To feel you slip beyond that point of control or reach, to have actually swallowed so large an object is an amazing feat, but to feel you disappear down my throat is an incredible, indescribable sensation. Once you are there, I do not want you to leave me. I want to hold on to that special, exquisite feeling forever, but alas, I have to breathe, and upon moving away and feeling you come out of my throat, it seems you come out forever—that the sheer length and width of you and having had you there, even momentarily, is an impossibility. The sensation afterward is much like orgasm. I cover my ears because I feel so excruciatingly sensitive to sound. I touch the outside of my neck and upper chest because it seems as though I can still feel you there. The sides of my throat are so sensitive to the width of you, and already I want you there again, over and over, and this time you go down easier because by now you are so well lubricated from the moisture of my throat. You slip down easier now, easier and deeper, until I almost want to risk the danger of taking all of you, which is impossible because of the very beautiful size of you. But the relaxed movement, the trust—I am breathing properly now which allows easier passage . . . I want you there forever. The sensation is new and special and shared with no one else. I want you there always. Breathing seems a small sacrifice to trade for the feeling.

Jasmine Carrietté

November 22, 1976

Dear Thomas,

I meant every word of what you just read, and although it speaks well of one dimension of our relationship, something about it kept bothering me. My valuing of you involves so much more than the sexual. You and I had been discussing it that day, and I had tried to express verbally to you how much you meant to me. I never got my point across because, somehow, we kept ending up in the bedroom while I was trying to explain to you, that for the first time in the entire relationship, I was at long last willing to give up the best and most satisfying sexual experience I had ever had, if indeed it was what was keeping us from being friends and loving each other. I was trying to express what you mean to me: that I value you sexually; but, ultimately, I value you even more greatly than that. You would hear none of it and tried to tell me no one was that valuable to someone else and insisted I did not know what I was talking about.

That made me mad because I knew how important you were, yet for one of the few times in my life, I felt at a loss for words to express exactly in what way. Indeed, I *could not* express it. When I began to really think about it, I could not answer why, and then slowly the answers began to come.

Somehow, in all of the writing I had done, there was no real explanation of my valuing of you. You kept telling me it was not your thighs, and even though the shape, size, and feel of them is so aesthetically pleasing to me, I, too, know this alone is no reason for the dichotomy which has existed in the relationship. I often have felt as though I were locked in some sort of waltz of death with you: unable to love and accept you as you are, but unwilling to let or want you to go out of my life. One fact I have always known: I want to keep you forever for my friend. I knew you were incredibly important to me for some reason, but I was not sure why. Your own double personality does not warrant such devotion, and most certainly should not warrant such devotion from me. Then today, rereading my letter of November

21st and desiring to put in some phrase about the fact that you have given me, or returned to me, my Southern heritage, the tears started flowing and I began to remember Faulkner's *Old Man*. The man in the story wanted and sought the free-floating buoyant space and freedom of the water. But also, some part of him longed for the solid ground, and he eventually reached the swamp, both land and water; and the dichotomy of reaching for and desiring both security and freedom and gaining neither. Much where I see you as being, and then I knew why I loved you.

You have made it okay, have given me the right, have made it acceptable to me, to be a Southerner. You have made it something not to be ashamed of. You have allowed me forgiveness. For me, the traditional guilt of the white Southerner has been expiated by a Northern black man. I do not mean I was not ready to be pardoned; but, my own trip home, my own willingness to finally put to rest some of my own ambivalence about my heritage was aided by you. Your very strong maturity about keeping what is valuable from the past and discarding what is not has been a help to me. I can keep my Creole cooking, Baptist gospel hymns, and warmth with people without accepting also the racist, bible-thumping demagogue. I need not be ashamed of being a Southerner ever again. You gave me that freedom. Not only to be sexually expressive—and I shall never devalue that, it is marvelous—but, more than that, you helped release the guilt and the burden of being a part of a particular group of people who treated others wrongly in a most severe way. They took their lives. It was a shame and a guilt I could not let go of. You would think I was smart enough to have known I alone was not responsible and could not pay the entire debt; but, it took a black man from Indiana to help me see that, and that is why I shall always love you. It is a very special gift that you alone were able to give me. I knew you had done something wonderful for me besides make beautiful love to me. I knew I valued you in a special way for something on a higher plane of friendship. But until today, I never knew what it was. Thank you most of all for helping me to see that it is okay to be from the South and that I need no longer carry all of the sins of the past on my shoulders, but rather take the good part of that heritage and enjoy it and discard the rest.

I do, Thomas Trout, truly love you, both sexually and as a friend who has given me a very great gift—a gift of freedom. Until you have walked in *my* shoes, do not discount the significance of the gift.

Jasmine

A Casualty of Love

"Diana Markus, please."
   "Just a moment."
   "Diana, do you know my Blue Cross insurance number?"
   "Jazz? What's the matter?"
   "Nothing serious."
   "Where are you?"
   "Lahey Clinic."
   "Why?"
   "I'm just having a chest X-ray."
   "What for?"
   "I think something might be broken."
   "What happened?"
   Cupping my hand over the phone, "I can't talk now. I'm in the lobby of the emergency room. People are all around. I'll tell you about it later. I don't have my Blue Cross card. I know how efficient you are; I thought you might know it."
   "I have it written in my address book. Hold just a minute."
   I looked up and the admitting nurse was assessing me with a quizzical expression. I looked back at the floor, smiling to myself.
   "Jazz, here's the number. And you wait right there after they take care of you. I'm coming to pick you up."
   "Diana, don't be ridiculous. Don't you dare leave work for this. I'm perfectly fine. I can drive myself home when I'm through. I'm supposed

to give a speech to the New England area directors at the Marriott in Wellesley at ten o'clock. I'll call you tonight and explain. I'm okay."

"If you're so okay what are you doing in the emergency room? I'll see you in about forty-five minutes."

"Diana, I just wanted to be sure nothing was broken. Really, I'm okay."

She hung up on me. I knew she'd be here. She was that kind of friend. When I decided to go for directorship in my company, she came to me and said, "You just go do whatever you need to do to build your business. You do the flashy stuff and throw all the paperwork on your desk. I'll be your secretary and assistant. I'll set up your office, your files, keep all your records, pay all your bills, tote and fetch, and set up the meeting room at the country club and hotel every week. I'll be your gofer. That's the role I'm happiest in—organizing, behind the scenes. You shine and I'll support. And in return, when you become successful, I want to work for you full-time." And that is what she did. We had been friends for over ten years. Diana is sixteen years younger than I, and we don't think alike about anything—not about men, or sex, or politics, or religion or social issues, or war, or governments. Nothing. I am never sure why, but there is a bond of love and friendship between us that has been one of the most sustaining of my life. We care about one another's welfare. It is good.

The nurse took me into a room off the side corridor. We both stood, she with a clipboard, filling out a form. "Where do you think you're injured?"

"Somewhere in the upper chest cavity."

"Why do you believe it's there?"

"That's where I hurt."

"Did you receive an injury?"

"Yes, but it wasn't intentional."

"What happened?"

"My lover and I were just playing around, and he hugged me a little too hard. He didn't mean to. Sometimes men don't know their own strength."

"Did he hit you or shove you?"

"Of course not." Suddenly, I realized she thought I was a battered woman. Knowing how the injury occurred, I laughed to myself. She continued probing. I understood her reluctance to believe my story, but there was no way I was going to tell this young woman how the injury really took place. She put me in a waiting room and I sat in the skimpy paper shirt open down the back and was cold. Waiting, I listened to the agony going on around me—people screaming in pain, children crying—and felt foolish for being here for such an absurd reason.

Finally, the doctor arrived. He had me hold my arms straight up, high over my head, as he carefully felt for broken ribs. I knew that was not where the injury had occurred, if indeed there was damage. He found no broken ribs. I put my arms down and with some reluctance explained to him no one had hugged me too hard. The weight had come from on top of my chest. Tom and I were making love. As he sat lightly across my chest while I performed fellatio on him, we got a little too exuberant and slipping, he allowed too much weight to fall on me. We heard the sternum crack; it sounded like a rifle shot. Tom stopped to ask if I was all right and I nodded without hesitation. I heard the sound in some deep inner recess of consciousness, but the intense sexual feeling of the moment far outreached any feeling of pain. The following morning we made love again.

It was only later, when sex no longer masked the pain, that I rolled over in bed, felt my chest wall cave in, and screamed. As I dressed for my lecture, every move became more excruciating, and I got frightened that whatever was broken might puncture my lungs.

"It sounds like you have a really good, vibrant, healthy sex life," said the doctor.

"That I do."

"It's wonderful to see at your age. I hope I'm as fortunate. You probably did separate the sternum from the breastbone. There's only a lot of cartilage holding it together. I'm going to schedule you for an X-ray so we'll be sure. There isn't much we can do for it except get you off your feet and I'm going to put you on Demerol for three days. The pain will be pretty intense, but I don't want to use the drug for a longer period of time if we don't have to. Let's just say you're a casualty of love." He wrote in my chart, and I knew the story would spread through the clinic, providing amusement for their solemn industry.

Waiting for the nurse to take me to X-ray, I could hear the man in the next room screaming constantly as they tried to pull his shoulder back into place. Diana walked in and we burst out laughing as she shook her head and smiled.

"Only you."

We tried to be more serious. Our hilarity was not appropriate to the setting, but we couldn't contain ourselves. Diana's acerbic wit was at its best on such occasions. "If this is how you look, I'd hate to see what happened to Tom after straddling your chest. Don't kid me, you weren't making love, your chest wall finally gave way from carrying that weight around all these years."

The nurse came to take me to X-ray, and looking at my chart and then up at the sign on the X-ray room door that said "If there is any possibility you might be pregnant please inform the staff before you have an X-ray." She said, "I normally wouldn't ask someone your age, but considering the reason for the X-ray, maybe I better ask if there is any chance you might be pregnant."

Tom left town that night for a quickly manufactured business trip to Washington. I told most people I had fallen on the stairs and hit my chest against the railing as I fell. He returned five days later as I was holding a sales meeting at the house. Diana walked in early to set up and greeted Tom, "Hello, crusher."

Christmas Eve, 1976

When I was young I'd always wanted to cook a roast and eat all the crisp outside part myself, put it back in the oven and get the outside crisp again—do it over and over and just keep eating the crisp part until the roast was gone. I thought as soon as I had a house of my own, when I was the wife and mother, that would be the first thing I'd do. I never did it. In my married life I have had three homes, two husbands, and two children. I have lived many places as a single woman, but I have yet to cook that roast and eat the crisp outside all by myself. Somehow, it lost its attraction as I got older. But whatever that represented to me—the ability to do as I pleased, and to eat only the parts that tasted best to me, to do what I wanted to do and not what I should do—that, I finally accomplished.

At forty-three, I realized relationships involve unequal power. I wish it was different, but since I could not change that fact, I wanted to be the one with the power. I realized for the first time that I did not always get everything I wanted. In earlier years I had convinced myself that I did, when, in fact, I had only allowed myself small dreams. I had been back in the dating world exactly nine months when this new awareness was thrust upon me. It was Christmas Eve, 1976.

As my friend Marsha commented later, there was something especially cruel about Tom's phone call coming on Christmas Eve, even if he were Jewish—which he wasn't.

"Jazz, I just wanted to let you know I'm going to be at the candlelight service with Betty."

"You can't be serious."

"Look, you got mad last time because you heard it from someone else. I thought I was doing the right thing by calling, but if you're going to be like this, I won't warn you."

"Tom, I'm standing here in my long red gown. My friends and their children are coming with me to the service. They know I go with you. You got out of my bed this morning, and tonight, thirty minutes before the service, you tell me you're coming with another woman?"

"I'm not coming with her. I'll be sitting with her. I'll be attending a party afterward to which we are both invited."

"You'll be sitting with her but you won't ever sit with me in church?"

"I explained I was trying to protect you."

"Protect me? And what are you doing now?"

"Jazz, I don't know what you want me to do. I knew this would happen. What happened to the woman who said to me 'I want no limiting relationships'?"

"I really can't talk about this right now. Janice is at the door. Thanks for the warning." I hung up, already numb.

I went to that candlelight Christmas service with my friends. The church was so crowded I never even saw Tom until I was leaving. He always sat near the back, and I sat a little more than half way up in an aisle seat, so I could see and hear everything that was going on. I held my head high that night (regally, I hoped) and my friends were at my side.

The service was lovely and joyful, I suppose. I really don't know. I had a bottle of Valium left over from an automobile accident I'd had two years earlier. I took four pills before I left home and planned on getting drunk when I returned. Drinking was not recommended with the pills, but I didn't care.

There was so much I didn't understand about being single. I thought Tom was one of the finest, kindest, brightest men I had ever known. How could he be both those things—that and this? How could I think him kind when he pulled stunts like this? I smiled through the service, there was no way I was going to let him see how his words and actions affected me. As my friends and I were leaving, we met Tom on the sidewalk of the snow-covered church lawn.

Grinning, hands in pockets, a sheepish little-boy look on his face although fifty years of age, he ventured, "Jazz, fancy seeing you here."

"Hello, Mr. Trout. You remember Janice and Carolyn."

"Most certainly. And how are you ladies?" Shaking their hands, with Janice visibly unwilling to do so yet not wanting to embarrass me, Tom turned to make some joking comment to their children. My friends quickly walked away and left us alone.

I reached up to hug him and brush his cheek with a kiss as I said, "Merry Christmas, Thomas Trout." I walked away before he could see the tears in my eyes. I caught up with my friends. Janice was furious.

"How could you be nice to that man? He chops you off at the knees and you smile. Are you crazy?"

"I never want him to know it matters."

"White women are crazy. There's not a black woman in the world that would put up with that shit. That's why black men date white women. You have so much guilt, you let him treat you like garbage. You think you're appeasing some past sin? How can you be so dense?"

"I love the man. What can I tell you? You want me to hang myself because of that?"

"You seem to be doing a pretty good job of that without my urging. How can you talk about love in the same breath with this man? He's evil. He's purposefully manipulating you. Do you think it's insignificant you're a lily-white Southerner?"

"Janice, you're so hard and bitter. Just because you've had a tough life, don't translate everything that's happened to you into racial terms for everyone else."

"Jazz, you're my friend, and I'm only going to say this once then we'll drop it. Because I'm black, I have a clearer picture of what's happening. This relationship has nothing to do with love. There is no way in this century, in this country, and especially between you and Tom, that this can have anything to do with love. I don't expect you to believe me now, but someday maybe you will. You're smarter than this. It's Christmas and I love you. You're my friend and I'd like to cut his heart out. Enough said. Let's go home and celebrate. We brought eggnog."

I hated her for what she said, and knew she was wrong. But thank God for friends. I took four more Valium that night on top of the alcohol. I slept. It was the worst Christmas I ever remember. I drank champagne all Christmas Day. Charles, my second husband, whom I had divorced earlier that year, picked me up to have Christmas dinner with old friends in the neighborhood where we had raised my children from my first marriage. That alone brought back enough sad memories. Did the pain never end, the compiling of pain upon pain? Was this all there was ever to be? I had felt such unbearable grief before my breakup with Charles. Did it go on eternally? Valium and booze got me through that Christmas. I had always liked Christmas. I didn't get depressed over Christmas like other people I knew. I was an incredible optimist. For what reason exactly, I was not sure. Certainly nothing from my childhood gave me any right to be optimistic, but here I was, unchanged, except for the drinking. I had lived a pretty sheltered existence in terms of my relationship to the world: Graduation Day. Thomas Trout would teach me a lot of things. Mostly they would be about myself.

From Diana's Perspective

Thomas had not heard a word Jazz said. Nothing changed about their relationship, and every time Jazz tried to discuss it, Thomas listened and responded in some sort of double speak language all his own. Words meant different things to Thomas than they did to the rest of the world, so it made communication nearly impossible. He had his own philosophy about how life should be lived and it worked great for him, but pretty much, the nearest I could tell, wreaked havoc on the lives of those closest to him. His mother died when he was eight, his father when Thomas was thirteen.

Thomas's wife had spent most of their twenty-one years of marriage in a mental hospital while he raised their two children and built a business. His son grew to manifest the same disease his wife had: schizophrenia. In those years, the early fifties, schizophrenia was attributed to the family, not brain chemistry. It was hard to discern just exactly what the problem with Tom was, because basically he was such a good, kind man. Yet, he seemed to destroy women. Why? I didn't know, watching, how much was attributable to Jazz herself and her personality, and how much was directly related to lapses in Tom's own makeup. It was Jazz's excessiveness and great capacity for enjoyment, matched by her great capacity for grief, which endeared her to her friends. Not that there is anything wrong with wringing each drop of emotion out of an experience, but sometimes she overdid it and exhausted her friends in her demand that they experience things at the same level of intensity.

Jasmine Carrietté

In the spring of the year I lived with Jazz, 1976, she would meet me in the yard as I got home from work and quite literally drag me from one lady slipper to another. Her yard, at the edge of the woods, was filled with lady slippers, and it was not enough that I admire one of them but rather I should appreciate how rare they were and extol the beauty of each individual blossom. This, before I could even change clothes.

The exasperation of driving around New Hampshire or Vermont with her during fall foliage required an admiration of each tree we passed ad nauseum. After the thousandth tree she declared a must-see, I just pretended to look while keeping my eyes on the road.

Jazz's long-term friends had to pace themselves. Her enthusiasm for life could be the most exhilarating thing in the world, but also, at times, required a great deal of patience. She, already in her forties, still possessed the wonder and awe of a child presented each day with a New World and she sincerely believed that God, or someone, had created it expressly for her enjoyment. It was delightful to watch, but also, at times, made me wonder why nothing brought me quite the same pleasure.

April 14, 1987

Jazz:

You said your adult writing assignment is to produce an objective portrait of yourself. While I can understand why you would find that challenging (the many facets of you!), I don't understand why this has suddenly become *my* assignment. Can you really at this stage of your life have so little feel for how other people see you? Surprising. Well, you asked.

I've known you so long I think of you as whole—not as an assemblage of parts and quirks. You're asking me to divide up my whole image of you and to try to remember the first impression you made on me and the idiosyncrasies that make you *you*. I'll try.

You have a classic face—oval shaped, aquiline nose, wide intelligent eyes of medium blue, which look more gray when you are tired. My mother always says she watches your mouth when you talk—that you have a very pretty mouth. You have good cheekbones and your face is very sculpted looking when you are at your best weight. Even when heavier it is exceptional—arresting. Your honey-color hair always looks great pinned up because it emphasizes the shape of your face and your classic profile.

You have always penciled your eyebrows in an upward direction on the outer ends. A good move because it makes your eyes look at once very clever and a little wicked.

Your voice is particularly pleasant to a Northerner. A nice, modulated woman's voice—not chirpy or harsh. You slur your words when you're tired as if you were drunk—you're not. When we talk on the phone and you're tired, I have to concentrate to catch all the words. Your voice goes up and down the scale when you speak in a way that our flat, often monotone Northern voices do not. Southerners and Englishmen tend to do that scale run. I like it.

Do you remember Bill Randall telling you in annoyance to please stop addressing him as "Bill Randall" during all of your conversations where anyone else would simply call him Bill? You do that (then more than now) when you talk to people—calling them by their full name. You don't do that to me. "Diana Markus" doesn't roll off the tongue so much. Or maybe you only full-name menfolk. I haven't noticed that bias, but it might be there. You explained to Jonathan that two-naming was a Southern habit. Is it? You always say "Tom Trout" for Tom Trout, making his whole name into a first name in a way. I personally think this is a nice habit—saying the entire name and fully recognizing the whole person.

Your carriage is impressive in large part because of your large parts. But that's not all of it. You don't slump (even though you've told me what an effort it is to carry double-D breast weight with your bra straps pressing into your shoulders). You always stand erect and your neck is long—or appears to be—because you hold yourself so well. I met you in the mid-seventies and your bra made no concession to the natural bras or no-bra look that had by then been popular for some time. As your friend, I know that's because you needed firm structural support, and that only came in bras that tend to make one look more, ah, apparent. For years you wore that Sno-Flake brand bra and it held you up, pointed, so that no one would ever guess you were ambivalent about your breasts. They preceded you into a room. And no baggy sweaters for you. With your large breasts and amazingly small waist, all five foot six of you, you stopped traffic.

Your eyes are always *interested* and involved in what's going on. There is nothing hesitant about you, even when you walk into a new crowd, a new situation. You act like you just walked into *your* party, and you're there to enjoy yourself. No wonder everyone gravitates to you, especially people who aren't as confident. You seem to assume people will like you and you don't change who you are in a crowd or one-to-one. I particularly admire that about you.

Although you like people, you don't hesitate to brand a fool a fool. Your sometimes scathing (acid mouth—who called you acid mouth?) assessments of the jerks you encounter are a nice balance to your mainly positive, people-liking good nature. As opposed to my Pollyanna boss, you recognize that there are nasty people, scoundrels, and bores out there and you know them when you meet them. My boss meets them and assumes they had a rough childhood and they therefore deserve extra kindness and attention from him. You are not a saint in that way, but are realistic about people while being warm and generous. At least toward your women friends. I think toward your lovers you are extremely demanding and not so forgiving.

You are witty and entertaining, intelligent, involved. Intuitive. Verbal. You tell a good story. You have extremely accurate recall for events and for conversations. You can repeat, years later, conversations that I was privy to, and although I couldn't have repeated them myself, I know your memory of what was said is true and very detailed. With your help I remember that a past conversation unfolded in just those words. What I don't always agree with is your *interpretation* of what was said or what transpired. Nevertheless, you do have great insight into people, what motivates them, and their true character.

Getting back to your "presence": your Dolly Parton figure and confident air remind me of the busts of women that used to adorn the old sailing ships. Head up, all chest and chin, going into the wind. That's the way you sail through crowds—all forward thrust. You carry that same thrust into your friendships. You demand, draw out, force participation on *your* level. You don't diminish your demands to fit your audience. When we meet after long absences I know you will often start our conversations by saying "Tell me everything!" or "Start talking!" You make one "engage" as you are engaged. That's great for me, since I am less open and usually need a jump-start.

You are impatient. Didn't your sister say you step into other people's space way before they are ready? That is true. You have strong likes and dislikes and are not uncertain about much. People react that way to you, too. They think you are wonderful or they avoid you. You say you'd rather sit on the wrong side of the fence than sit astride it undecided. Make a decision. Stand for something. I never met anybody who feels lukewarm about you. You are an exhilarating friend. You can be an exhausting friend.

You have a very expressive eyebrow—one that lifts or frowns while the other brow remains steady. That animated brow is very good at expressing skepticism, disapproval, or just plain interest.

Your laugh is good—spontaneous and not held back. You have a hair-trigger ear for racist words as a result of your background, but as our black friends have often pointed out, you get offended for black people where a black person wouldn't. Remember when you and I, with our respective black boyfriends, were watching one of those television epics. Was it *Roots*? You just about ruined it for the rest of us with your tears and insistence (in the middle of the show) on discussing it with the men: How could they watch this? Wasn't it just too painful? How did it make them feel? You finally went upstairs in tears, too disturbed by the program and, more specifically, by our black friends' calmness, to watch any further.

You know how to listen when you want to. You sit very still and simply nod encouragement, are very patient and don't interrupt. You are not patient at all when you are excited about something. Then you interrupt, comment, ask questions and make it difficult for me to tell a story with anything like coherence. But when you are simply thoughtfully engaged and listening, no one I know does it better.

You used to make a person pay for your patience and attention by then sharing all of your opinions and observations about what your friend just said, few holds barred, always smart and incisive. I admit you have mellowed in this regard. Your tactic now is to tease me with your withheld opinions, assuring me that you have some, and reminding me that in the old days you would have bludgeoned me with them, but now you won't share those insights unless I ask you to do so. Naturally, after some hesitation I always ask. I've got to say I miss your pushy insistence that I grow and become enlightened along with you at your pace rather than your giving me a choice whether to hear your opinion. Your pushy insistence was a funny and endearing part of your character and I have had to adjust to a more mellow, less crusading you. I guess there is something very nice about being the object of someone's crusade, or at least being in the ranks behind the crusader witnessing her charge.

You are blunt. Honest. Intolerant of stupidity. Loving. Fun. Challenging. Unique.

Is this sufficient?

Love you,

Diana

January 29, 1977
Journal—early morning

Tom,

    You lie by my side, inches away, through the wall, and how I long to reach out for you: to touch you, to touch you in some way which will be irrefutable, to reach your soul as you have mine, to leave some indelible blot on your life as you have mine, to touch the marrow of your innermost being as you have mine—for you to know I AM.
    You touched my life in such a special way. I will remember you always. I miss you so. How I long to be snuggled in your arms now: loving you, touching you; but it can never be, and to admit that is to admit failure again to myself. I could not make it work for me. Could not make you love me. Could not make you care or know that I was different or had a soul or felt the hurt. I could not make ME matter to you. I wanted so very much to matter.

Jasmine Carrietté

January 31, 1977

Tom,

And because writing is my skill, you factitiously disregard my feelings as being of little value, of the moment, unimportant. Because it is easy for me to be verbal, somehow you equate that with being insincere. Your logic is misguided and unfortunate.

Not once since I have known you have I felt other than intensely about you—sometimes love, sometimes hate, but always it was intense.

Bear with me through these letters until I work out my feelings, and gradually with time and patience begin to get you out of my system. You don't even have to read them if they become a burden to you. I just need to say what I feel to work through the pain of the loss of the joy of you. It gets easier every day; but, for now, this moment, I still miss you so.

Jazz

Desire Makes the Difference

March 18, 1977
For Thomas Trout

Longing

Oh, the sweet pain of waiting to be touched by you.

The day has been spent at the peak of passion—in hold.

Stretched to its highest limits—continuously.

Held there by memories of other days and other touchings

and how you made me feel,

again, and again, and again.

The joy and delight of you is unique,

unsurpassable.

I'll wait as long as I must.

The reward is worth the effort and the tension.

But please my love, come soon.

Jasmine Carrietté

April 4, 1977

Dear Tom,

I wanted to convey to you how very much your visit on Saturday meant to me. If I could have had a choice, I would have preferred to remain your lover. But since we could not make that relationship work for us without the destruction of our own inner peace, it then became very important to me, because of the specialness you have been in my life, that we at the very least remain good, dear friends.

Alas, I was beginning to think we were destined to be unsuccessful at that also. I love you and I want you to continue to be a part of my life. Thank you for working at it and making it possible.

Jasmine

June, 1977
Journal

    If only all affairs could always be a beginning, a renewal, a rejuvenation, a joy, a giving, a strength. If only the pain never came, the pain of losing me to others. The pain of giving up me for him. The pain of suddenly knowing I can no longer fill my own needs. That dreaded feeling of dependence, which is necessary if one is to share who they truly are, but independence so very, very difficult to recapture, once that person is gone out of your life and there is no one to touch. How really very marvelous if we, as women, as people, could learn to give without losing. Somehow, I wonder, if way back there, or finally, I never got enough to give and still keep me.

January 25, 1978
Journal

    I am really going out of my mind today. I feel extremely nervous and jumpy. Bored to death with my job, which I usually love. Tired, restless, not feeling well physically. Eating a bit too much and beginning to feel stuffy, but still hungry and not satiated. As though food were not what I was really seeking, or at least it does not prove to be the answer. The appetite is there though, and I think shall be until Thomas Trout is resolved in my life. My God, what do I really feel about him? Right now, it is as though I wish I never had to see him again.
    I am tired of not knowing. Had just as soon let it go. Do not wish to expend the effort to resolve it. Feel there is now and never will be any reward for all of my effort. I am tired of giving to him. I want something for me. When I cried after Jim made love to me, I knew. It was just like it was after John first touched me. Only then, when someone is giving to me, do I realize how drained I am from giving constantly to Tom and never receiving from him. Basically, I think I am a generous person. But when one takes as much as he takes from me, both emotionally and economically, I finally wear out. I have nothing to give to anyone else. Only when someone else finally gives to me do I realize how depleted I am. I think, ultimately, I really don't want to be involved with Tom again. I have made the break from him during the past two weeks. I had just as soon let it lie.

March 21, 1978

Dear Tom,

You said put it down on paper, so here goes. I guess what really angered and hurt about you saying I was becoming like all of your other women, is that there was some degree of truth in it. Unfortunately, we disagree about the cause of that. I, of course, think it is you who sets up the failure in the relationship, and you naturally think it is a smallness on my part. Regardless, although I value having you to touch in my life, indeed value so very many things about you, I find the relationship has now reverted to the same bad one we had in the beginning.

Tom, for the few months we had, from the end of August until the middle of January, I am grateful. They were beautiful and good and what we should have always enjoyed. I felt truly valued and cared for. I will always remember that time and how lovely it was. When you treat me as you do now, I become less sure that I am cared for and turn into something I don't like. I am not basically a clutching, demanding kind of person who trades favor for favor or even counts them; but when I feel unloved as I do now, I change and indeed do become a very unattractive person. I don't like it and refuse to allow that to happen to me again.

I don't have the answer, but I do know I don't want to continue the relationship anymore along the lines in which it is presently going. Talking does not seem to help. Saying we are going to stay out of each other's lives does not seem to help. No matter what we say, we seem to keep ending up together. I truly like and enjoy other men, but they can never be you to me. You are special and I make no effort to deny that; but I refuse to be dragged down into this inevitable sick relationship again. If you can't say you love me, get the hell out of my life. I'll miss you, but go. Understand I do not want you to go; but neither do I want to stay in the relationship as it is.

Jazz

Jasmine Carriette

January 24, 1979

Dear Tom,

How very, very good it was to hear your voice. I do love you so. At the sound of you, I was inundated with a flood of pleasant memories. The balance of the day found me feeling so vulnerable and scared. All of the wounds of our parting of three months ago were suddenly left gaping and raw again. My caring is still so far from casual and always shall be. I love and miss you so.

Tom, I barely survived the holidays. I have done a lot of dumb things in my life, but breaking up with you just before the holidays has to rank near the top for sheer idiocy. If we had made it together, off and on, for nearly three years, a couple of more months couldn't have hurt and it sure would have helped cheer the yuletide season. All of the invitations to parties and dinners I kept receiving for "us," the Christmas cards addressed to Jasmine and Tom, etcetera. None of that made dealing with the loss of you in my life any easier; but, as always, bit by bit, striving every day just to survive one day at a time, I finally am beginning to heal (although ever so slowly it seems).

And then Bill's call, your illness, and my phone call to you has suddenly dumped all of those devastating feelings upon me again in full force. It has been a painful night and day for me. (A different kind of pain from yours.) It hurts very badly to know someone I love is seriously ill and suffering. It is only natural that I should want to be there with you to know you are all right, to be able to touch you and feel you breathe, to sit quietly by your side, or just to hold your hand. It is a small matter but so significant when I feel concern about your welfare from such a distance; yet, I would never violate or interfere with your relationship with Gertrude. She is there for you when you need her. She has helped in so many ways. She gives you much and you are fortunate to have her. It is so frightening to be ill and alone. Although I would give anything just to look at you and know you are going to be okay, nothing could be more disastrous for me right now.

After you left me I did "date" several people for a short while. There were a lot of things wrong with those experiences and finally, after forty-five years, I was able to give myself permission simply not to respond to men for a while. I do not know how long this will last, but believe me Tom, it was like laying down a very heavy burden. First, I had to relate to my father (no easy task), then Allen, then immediately Charles. For three months after Charles, I was alone; but, from that time on, there was you. Out of a total of forty-five years, there have only been three months of my life when I was not responding to men. I have more often than not thought of myself as rather independent and not buying in to a lot of our training and teaching about pleasing men. Now, when I realize how solidly I bought that whole package, it scares me. So being quiet and alone and giving myself time to heal has been a very right decision for me at this time. It is a time and a place I need: to grieve for the loss of you; to be quiet and know myself and who I am and what I want; to be still and realize your value. I do want what we had—with someone who wants to share that with me. The comfortableness of you is something I shall long for, for a while I suppose.

Tom, you made me feel so special, unique, as though I had something to offer, that I was unusual. I felt cared for by you—some would call it loved. You made me feel I had something to contribute. I don't think I shall be alone always because there is so much I want to give, but I also wish very much to be at peace should I be alone for the rest of my life. That is what I am working on now. First, to heal from the loss of you. Second, to be at peace with aloneness. I am sure eventually I shall be successful at both. Then perhaps, and only then, can I trust myself not to ever believe I am happy with a three-year relationship where I am never taken out. No wonder you could not trust me; it had to be obvious to you long before it was obvious to me that I was lying about being satisfied that you never acknowledged I was your girlfriend.

You are so smart, but I am learning and I shall make it eventually. However, right now, in my aloneness, and trying to grow, when I learned how quickly you were back entrenched with Gertrude again, let me tell you, sir, it hurt. I felt even more rejected. As though your relationship with me had meant nothing and it is she you really love—so many insecure feelings which aren't even relevant. I am okay today and thinking more rationally, but it was a brief setback, and my first reaction was the old desire to be in the arms of someone else to forget the pain. That never solved anything before, and today my resolve not to respond to men is as strong as ever.

As I talked with you and remembered all of the fun we had, I want so very badly to be able to be your friend and share all of those things again. I have so many new friends you would love and enjoy so much. Janice Carter is the alto we have been looking for, for years, to sing with us. She has a beautiful voice. She has worked for me for several months now. She is from Dallas, a Christian, and knows all of the hymns. She and her husband have a beautiful home in Wellesley, and we sang many songs together over the Christmas holidays, wishing for your beautiful bass voice and sunny disposition to join us. You would love their home and hospitality, that extra bit of graciousness of the Old South. I have so many good new recipes from her. She wishes she could have known you. I speak of you with such joy; they want to know you, too. Patsy is a new, young girl (twenty-one) working with me now. Oh Tom, I worked so hard to get her here. She is absolutely fantastic. She is pure pleasure to have around, and the kind of person you would adore. I wish you could know her. June and Ken called on Christmas and cannot believe they will not be able to be with both of us, together, to share good times on their visit here in the spring. It is still so difficult to think of my life without you. No one wants to share heartache. The times I miss you the most are when I feel joyful about something. I still think of everything good in terms of wanting to share it with you. Christmas Eve at Louise and Frank's lovely home; the fabulous food and fascinating people I met I wanted you to know, too.

God, soon that must change; but, for now, sometimes, I feel it never will. If sex is what causes the pain, then it seems we could give up the sex and just simply love each other. Unfortunately that is not a possibility for me right now. I am so strongly attracted to you. Inevitably, I know, I would eventually touch you again. There is no joy on this earth equal to that of lying all night in your arms. Yet, you can cause me such pain. I know you value me, but I could never reconcile that with being left at home while you went to the Cape every weekend alone or took another woman. I would love nothing better than to be able to be your friend.

For now, nothing is further from being within the realm of possibility for me. I cannot go from being your lover to being your friend. I simply cannot, so in order to protect ME—I shall stay away. Know however that you are loved and valued and longed for as I have loved and longed for and valued no other.

I went to Baton Rouge right after Christmas, and Tom, let me tell you, there is something magic, really magic about a grandbaby. He is not only physically adorable, he has such a marvelous disposition. He never meets a stranger and will go to anyone. He laughs so winningly at everyone. He is such a charmer. He is surrounded by a large family on the sides of both parents, so someone is always holding him. There is so much love and warmth and support in his life, and it was good to see. They are good parents who thoroughly enjoy him. I am so glad. My visit with Bradley was momentous. We talked for hours and he has turned out to be such a fine man. I am so proud of him, and our relationship is such a good one again. I had the best visit ever with Yolanda, and she has done some personal growing at last. Jessica is still happy with James and sends her love to you. She is praying for you during this illness and she hurts for us both. My mother is dying and should be in a nursing home within the next few weeks. She weighs 112 pounds and was once a very tall woman. Getting old is not easy.

Tripper is the same beautiful dog he always was. He is a comfort and a joy to me. He keeps me company so often. Diana stayed with him while I was away, and I felt it a real imposition to ask her to. He would not eat while I was gone and never left my side once I returned (still will not). I was sick on my return and he was quite confused because I never got out of bed. I am not sure I will be able to manage this summer alone and keep him. It will be a hard decision.

Work is still so good for me. My relationship with my boss is the one good male/female relationship of my life. He values me and has not vetoed one single thing I have attempted to do. That gives me an awful lot of support, but a lot of responsibility for being sure I am right, too. I am so glad for this one good peaceful part of my life. I feel I have a good future with the company. Our department is growing fast and that can mean only good things for me. I am still always late for work. I always blamed being late for work and being overweight on you, but

I was wrong. Although I am not screwing around with you or anyone else, I am still never on time. The weight, however, is better. Between dieting and being sick I have lost fifteen pounds and feel much better because of it.

Tom, I have said so much in this letter. I suppose it is my need to touch you in this time of illness. I remember one of my letters making you so angry once. I recall a similar response to one of Gertrude's. Please know how hard it is for me to remain silent right now. Choose those thoughts I have shared with you that you like and discard the rest as unworthy. Please realize the intent is well meant and give me some benefit of the doubt as I write from my own confused state.

I shall never come and interfere in your life, but please know my thoughts are with you. I am concerned for your well-being. I want so much for you to be well and strong and healthy again. I need for you to hear that I love you. I need for you to know you have but to pick up the phone and call me if there is anything I can do for you.

Would that I could kiss your wounds and be a part of your healing.

Jasmine

P.S. I read a book recently I want to share with you. I'll send it when I get a copy. Try to read it. We're both in there.

Strength—July 28, 1980

Dearest Sister,

I have been thinking of you so much this weekend. I tried to call you last night but unsuccessfully.

This weekend Michael and I went camping in New Hampshire. It was really lovely. Not too hot but warm enough so that the water felt really refreshing. Not humid, though, like when we were there. Not a single insect to bother you. Perfect. The moon was full as I went alone, late at night, to return the canoe to the boathouse. I cried remembering how you and I had paddled around and you did not want to go in because it was your last night and you never got to go canoeing. It was so beautiful, Jessica, with the moonlight on the water and the mountains in the background.

Michael did not want to go with me because he was afraid of the water at night. He did not want me to go either, but I left him saying, "I have been camping alone for four years now. I can take care of myself. I can do anything." And as I drifted out on the lake immersed in the beauty of the surroundings and my own thoughts of our times there together and wishing you were with me, I thought a lot about our dad. He did a lot of things wrong, Jessica, especially not protecting us from our mother; but the one thing he gave us was an ability to take care of ourselves. His love of the out-of-doors, the woods, being able to live and survive in a natural environment, is an incredible gift he gave us. Do you realize how few women our age could be left alone out-of-doors and make it? That ability and strength, I believe, carries over to other things as well. I am so glad we had the opportunity to grow up in the country. I think it important to our ability to survive and to feel at ease—at peace with strength.

Losing Tom has been hard. Not him especially, I don't miss him. I miss having someone like him. I dislike so many things about the way he treated me, but I would love to have adult male company, too. I share this with you for your thinking about Kenneth. Giving up the dream is the hardest part. I've only recently done it. I'm watching Cathy literally crippled physically with the effort of doing it, and I don't think I exaggerate that. I think she feels it, too, but can't help it yet and that is okay. Just crank it into your thought process regarding Ken. It is the loss of hope which is sad. The pain of losing him was over long ago. It is the emptiness of losing the dream that is the saddest.

I must get back to work—just needed to visit with you, if only in spirit.

I love you,

Jazz

The Ask

It was a cold January night, January 11, 1984; I'll never forget it. Tom was propped up in bed watching Ted Koppel on the eleven o'clock news. It was the last commercial, so I knew it was a safe time to bring it up. We never went to bed before one o'clock, and there was still plenty of time. I had been in my room under my electric blanket reading, trying to keep warm in this desolate house, feeling the deprivation not only from Tom but also from the cold. The lack of warmth is so bleak to me, even now. Nothingness. My room, at least, was comfortable. There was a warm blue carpet on the floor and antique printed wallpaper with matching curtains, old furniture with eight-sided tables which had elaborate but delicate legs, curlicues and knobs of rich woods, comforting to both the hand and the eye.

Tom's room by contrast was stark, forbidding, wallboard of a light gray, no curtains at the windows, not even shades, a bare bulb hanging from the ceiling. No one would believe this man had money. It was his choice to live this way. It was my choice to leave, finally. But I had this one last mission, from Lilly. She made me promise. I had to make a verbal contract with her when I entered therapy that I would make no changes in my relationship with Tom without us discussing it and agreeing on it first. It was so hard not to act impulsively. Impulsive, how could one call eight years impulsive? I waited as I told her I would, although many nights, arguments with Tom would have led me quite naturally to leave his bed. I stayed until I discussed it with Lilly as I had promised I would. Keeping my word was a point of moral character with me. I did it on this occasion in spite of my natural inclination to make hasty decisions, which might be harmful to my welfare later. But Tom had promised that we would talk tonight, so I approached him, already knowing the outcome, sure of what he would say, but understanding when Lilly said I needed the practice of asking for what I wanted.

Never, never, had I been able to do that. I was taught not only by word, but also by extreme example, that women—especially good Southern women—served their men. They asked for nothing, but rather manipulated in quite devious ways for everything. They had a lot of power, but not in any way that was attractive to me. I watched my mother seduce my father daily. It was not seduction for any fun or games, but a deadly ritual for power and control and money. Five days a week for as long as I can remember I heard my father counting out the items on his dresser "knife, nick, key, comb, watch." It wasn't actually a nickel; it was fifty cents. My mother never went to work outside the home a day in her life. My father worked until he died. But every payday he handed over his entire paycheck to my mother, and in exchange she doled out to him, five days a week, fifty cents. I was humiliated for him. Jessica and I were doled out equally twenty-five cents each for school lunch. We had to sign a form saying we were needy to receive free school lunches. Every kid in school did it but us. Kids whose families had lots more money than we did received free lunch, but it was a sticking point with my father. He refused to lie and say we were needy when we were not, so we—my sister and I—got the equivalent of my father's daily income to go out into the world with. I don't think my mother ever understood the humiliation of having only fifty cents in front of his friends, but she never understood, either, what it meant for her sisters or later her daughters to be employed outside the home. She never modified in later years what she expected in way of service from Jessica, even though Jessica held down a full-time job and took care of herself and our mother.

After our mother was dead, Jessica and I went through bags of quilting scraps our mother had saved for many years. We saw square after square of material which we remembered were dresses we had worn in school when we were small. Out of the many bags, we found two squares which we recalled were dresses of our mother's, but later, when we were grown and away from home, our mother would buy very expensive outfits and hide them for weeks from our father, only bringing out a piece at a time, a handbag here, a new hat there. He never complained about what she spent, and we never understood her need for deception. My father demanded and received hot meals on the table at certain times each day with no deviation, and he got them. He walked across the living room rug with muddy boots if he desired. Only kings never carry money. I got so many mixed messages about how a relationship was to be conducted between a man and a woman; I wasn't surprised that at fifty I was still trying to sort it out.

Service and lies and deception and manipulation had not prepared me for honesty and confrontation. To go into a man's room, even the man I had sex with every morning and every night, and to ask, bluntly, honestly, openly, for what I wanted or needed from him was a new and radical concept. At this point in time, I knew that he knew what I wanted, but Lilly said (and I knew she was right) I needed to ask. I needed the experience. I needed to know the world would not disappear or crumble when I asked and did not receive. I needed to know how to take care of myself by asking. I needed to practice now, on a relationship that was going nowhere, for a later one, which may have promise. I needed most of all to hear him say no, he could not give me what I wanted from the relationship. So I went into his room to ask. It was not an easy thing to do.

"You said we could talk tonight. Is this a good time? Are you ready?"

"Wait just a few minutes. This is almost over."

"It's over."

Grinning, "You really want to do this?"

"I do."

"You're never satisfied."

"Almost never."

"You know how I think."

"Yes, I do. I've heard you say often enough 'All women have the same mother.'"

"Right."

"Right. And I wonder who fathered the men? There's room for improvement there as well."

"Do you mind if I work while we talk?"

"I mind."

"You're serious about this, aren't you?"

"I'm serious, and it amazes me that you can't tell."

"What's to tell? We've had this same conversation for eight years."

"Not quite."

"Oh really, what's different?"

"I'm not sure I can explain it. I'm older and more tired for one thing. There's my work in therapy with Lilly for another. Don't ask me how or why, but I know in the deepest recesses of my soul it's different. I can't yet tell you what's different. Ask me a year from now, but let's talk about what I do know."

"You're sure you want to do this?"

"I'm sure."

"Jazz, why can't you leave well enough alone? If you were in paradise and everything was perfect, you'd want to rearrange one rose."

"Since I'm not even close to that, I'll risk it."

"Then go ahead."

"For eight years we've had an open relationship. That was your idea, and you finally convinced me to go along. It was what you wanted, and after I tried it, I discovered the sun still rose. I could love more than one person at a time, and making love with another man did not change my feelings for you. But no more. Finally, I've healed from my destructive divorce from Charles. I want, finally, a committed, caring relationship with you. I love you, Tom. I want more. I'm not sure yet that it means marriage, but I want a one-on-one, committed relationship. I find it ironic that your goodness to me, which has allowed me to heal and want more, may, because of your choices, exclude you from my life, but life is often like that—ironic. I find myself wanting to trust again, and it is because of you. It seems that may lead us to part, but I did not want to go, indeed was unwilling to go, without asking, even though I know your philosophy. I want a commitment from you, not for marriage. Right now I want a commitment of physical fidelity, and I want an agreement to spend two holidays a year with me, and occasional weekends. That is all. Not a lot by some standards, a great deal by yours. Before you answer I want you to know that if you cannot give that to me I intend to move out of your bed. I will never have sex with you again.

It does not mean I will not love you. It does not mean I will not want you. It does not mean I will not desire you. It means I will no longer act on any of those feelings."

Smiling, "This is blackmail."

"Not at all. This is honesty, and what a poor word choice for a black man."

"Jazz, you know I'm not a talker; I've never talked. Why don't you watch my actions instead?"

"I do."

"Then why isn't that enough?"

"I finally know I deserve more."

"Do you realize I have this same conversation with every woman I know?"

"Oh really."

"They all envy you. They'd like to exchange places with you."

"Would they really like to be the one living with you and receiving calls saying, 'Tell Tom when he comes for dinner just to come on in if I don't hear him. I'm down in the cellar painting.'"

That grin again. "You know I like to eat. I'll go anywhere if somebody feeds me. Like a stray dog."

"Let's get back to the subject at hand. Tom, we've broken up and gone back together so many times I'm not surprised you don't believe this occasion is different, but regardless, whether you believe me or not, if you can't give me the things I need, I'm leaving. I need a response. Part of the exercise of me having to ask is to hear you answer and know the world still revolves."

He was serious, finally. Did he know, too, understand, that this was different? "I don't want you to go, Jazz. You know that without asking. I'll miss you sexually. You're a very giving, generous woman. I don't want you to go, but I can't give you what you're asking for."

"Why not?"

"Because then you'll only want more. We're never satisfied. If we have ninety percent, it's the ten percent we don't have that seems outstanding, unbearable."

"You're probably right, but why don't you try me. We've made it eight years together because we both need so much freedom. We both want and need many other people and activities in our lives. We share so many good things. Why won't you even try?"

"I know the outcome. I've tried it before. It's always what I can't give that will be the one thing you'll want and then you'll leave me anyway, only angry."

"You tried? When?"

"With my wife."

"So you're letting me go. For two holidays and a few weekends, you'd lose all we share?"

"Commitment, don't forget commitment."

"You say one relationship is all you can handle at a time. With all the sex we have and at your age, I believe you're telling me the truth. I doubt you're laying many other women."

"But I want to know I can. It's mental. It's knowing I'm free to touch someone else should I desire to."

"That's funny. I always know I can. It's not something you give me. It's a gift I grant myself."

"But you know I don't limit you either."

"And you feel limited by me?"

"I would come to."

"God forbid. You said you'd miss me sexually. Is that all you'll miss?"

"That's all you're taking away. I'll still have everything else about you. Won't I?"

I sat at the foot of the bed. Tears filled my eyes. What an overwhelming sadness of two people who cared so much but were unable to reach one another. I got up, held him close, felt his warm, hard body next to mine, touched with my fingertips his velvet, black skin and knew that for years ahead there would be much darkness for me to pass through before this dear, wounded, lonely man was removed from my soul.

"I don't want to change, Jazz."

Jonathan Noble

Five months after I broke up with Thomas Trout I met a quite marvelous young man. We knew each other briefly, but I withdrew from that situation quickly. I realized I was repeating an all too familiar pattern. The timing was not right for either of us.

Three years later, in many ways it was. He has proved a dear, supportive friend throughout these years. He was thirty-seven at the time, self-employed, lived far away but traveled to Boston often on business. Because of the age difference, I knew the relationship was not going anywhere, but we love one another in positive, good, healthy ways.

I ended my celibacy with him that fall. He has helped me with so many of the sexual issues I could not possibly work out in theory with Lilly. Although he enjoys fellatio, he is unwilling to let me do all of the giving. It has been hard for me to learn to have normal sex, frontal, connected, face to face, to be kissed, the missionary position: a first for me in about thirteen years. I am such a strong woman. Given enough time I can and will eventually have my way with most any man. Finally, they get tired of struggling with me and just take. My pathology does not show unless you go to bed with me. Most men are happy to take.

Jonathan Noble was not. I will be eternally grateful to him for loving me enough to slowly and gently and patiently nurture in small ways until my ability to receive increased. It was glorious. Being well is so superior to illness. There is no future—no forever after which we were raised on—with Jonathan, but there will always be a love and a friendship.

Jasmine Carrietté

May 18, 1984

Dearest Jonathan,

It is now 1:15 p.m. and I am sitting by the edge of a pond in Carlisle in an area of woods and fields with an enormous rambling red barn and silo in the distance. The sun is bright. The day is clear.

And in my heart, there is a lightness I've never known before.

All morning I have ached to be alone so that I might write. There is a singular uniqueness to my experience with you and I'd so much love to convey exactly what that is. The difference.

My memories of last night seem almost too significant and sacred to commit to print. Like somehow verbalizing them will take away the magic and it will all dissolve and disappear much like fog lifting from a meadow. A vapor, untouchable, unable to be recaptured—as though even the audacity of trying will guarantee the loss of specialness.

But it is important to me to preserve and record forever the gains. A knowing I never had before. A realization I never knew was possible. A bonding I had never expected. A coming together finally of events in my life which allowed me to know with an unexpected surety that there is hope. That I do deserve to be loved the way you loved me.

Afterward, as we held one another, you said something like, "You paid so much attention to my needs that you almost denied your own." My therapist gives you an A++. She has been trying to get me to see that for months. You called me on it within a few hours.

Always, I have done in bed what pleases me. I am not phallically oriented because it pleasures you but because of the joy of having you in my mouth (and God you are beautiful), so I never knew the difference. I never knew there *was* a difference. I only knew how to express what I felt. I never had anyone care enough about me to require, or demand, or take delight in my joy, excitement, and response at being pleasured to the degree that you did, thus enabling our lovemaking to become such a mutual response.

Jonathan, I have never been touched by anyone the way you touched me. You have the longest, slimmest, most sensuous fingers, and I feel as though where you touch me my body becomes liquid, viscous—melting at the tips of your fingers. When my mouth became dry from hyperventilation, you covered it with yours and exchanged what imparted to me a seeming life-giving fluid. Life on this earth began in water, and to me there is something so earthy and sensual about moisture. I loved feeling throughout the night the copious abundance of your semen in my body.

But about your touching; there is a difference. No one, absolutely no one, ever held me, just me, not a part of my body the way you did for ages, before we ever proceeded to genital sex. Jesus, that makes one feel cared for! Like it is *me* you are connecting with, not my breasts or my vagina. You've spoiled me, Jonathan. I'll hate the way other men show affection now. I love, simply love the way you envelope me in your arms and hold me close for long periods of time. I begin to breathe so freely and all my pain is healed (and I had lots of pain before you touched me).

I'm writing this all very badly and perhaps the beauty of it should be left unspoiled by trying to verbalize the experience. One can't equate it. I just wanted you to know that no one ever cared about my feelings to the degree you did, or evidenced it. I want that. I need it. I deserve it; I'm discovering. I never knew it was possible before. I never knew there was a difference.

UNTIL YOU, THERE COULD BE NO JUXTAPOSITION.

Lest you misunderstand, I have had good lovers, superb in fact, sexual athletes. And many who did care that I enjoyed it, too, to a degree. But never ANY who touched and held and connected the way you do.

You learned technique perhaps, but *Playboy* does not teach how to value your fellow man. Few men I know value women the way in which you do, and that explains why you touch differently. Your touching is not altered because of sex or age.

I cannot believe that you entered my life and my body at exactly the stage when I was working on the issue of valuing myself, feeling I, too, deserve pleasure.

You speeded up the process one hundred fold. For me, therapy truly is the key. But life is the laboratory. Thank you.

Are you aware of the biblical practice of the "laying on of hands"? Truly I do feel healed. I shall value myself and my needs more, because one particular night, YOU DID. I love you for that.

I am so grateful you can risk being different.

Jasmine

May 30, 1984

Dear Jonathan,

We are both in the midst of such a painful, growing process. Perhaps had we met at a different time and place in our lives, one or the other of us would have had more to give. For now, the immediate present, we both need someone who can give to and understand us.

Normally, I do have much to give and could be a positive influence for growth in your life, but now, today, I must be learning hard lessons of my own; primarily, how to be open, vulnerable, receptive to those who want to give to me. For someone whose life has been built on power and control, there is nothing more frightening.

Meeting you is much like a supreme test. Never have I found in one person so many of the qualities I desire, and to walk away from that because it is an unhealthy situation is one of the most difficult things I have ever had to do.

Truly, Jonathan, I do love who you are. You stand for and are about everything I value. A willingness to communicate and work on issues, a willingness to grow and change. You, too, are on a search, a quest— to be otherwise is to become stagnant and in the truest sense "old." Your desire to bond, connect, in reality to touch another's life in some significant way, is something I have searched for always in a partner. And, of course, there is the physical . . . which satisfies some deep, previously untouched part of me.

I am grateful, truly grateful we met. My life is richer, more fully blessed because I've known you. No matter the outcome of your decision regarding meeting my needs, someday, at some other time and place, if I am lucky, perhaps the time will be right for us to share and touch to the detriment of neither. I hope so.

You have my fondness and best wishes for you and your life. May you find peace and joy in your struggle to know all of the good things a man like you deserves.

Work hard in therapy and in whatever you do, Jonathan. Don't sell yourself short. I am a bright lady and I am here to tell you: you are special, very, very, special.

I do love you,

Jasmine

August 8, 1984

Dear Jonathan,

How good to hear from you. I'm so excited about your business plans. I decided after our talk that the best thing I could do to help you in sales is to introduce you to my senior director. She has done it all. She has won everything this company gives away. She is a real superstar, but so unassuming. She is an interesting study with an unusual background. I've learned a lot from her.

Have you done much reading on the subject? Are you aware there is no profile to predict who will be successful at sales? That is why the turnover rate is so high. It is not predicated on IQ or any of the traditional qualities which make one successful, either academically or at other careers.

Your racing is going well, too. WOW! Life has so many options. Isn't it grand?

Jack said you found it difficult to call me. Why? I think I am so able to talk to. Is my perception wrong? If so, it would not be the first time. I had a therapist once who said to me, "Jasmine, your perceptions are all fucked up." So maybe I am not as easy to talk to as I assume. All I know is that I hunger for conversations such as I share with you. They meet a very real need of mine for intimacy and delight that even sex could never touch. I do believe that I have been starving intellectually. I plan to change that.

I have already started to read the bibliography for the writing seminar at Radcliffe in the fall and am enmeshed in many marvelous books on various subjects. I am reading for a course that will only accept fifteen people and that acceptance will be based on a writing sample. Keep your fingers crossed for me. I really want this one.

I am taking out an equity loan on my home and shall do lots of repairs, then re-rent it at a much better rate. My unit is finally working again which should bring us back productionwise after a very bad year. Tom and I seem to be relatively at peace as we go through more of our transition phase. Oh Jonathan, I have learned so much this year.

Jasmine Carrietté

I am not the same person I was six months ago. All in all, I feel life is wonderful and no small part of that has been the knowing of you. Thank you for your love and your friendship.

Do come to Boston soon. To talk. Preferably at a time when you can see my sales director work.

I love you,

Jazz

Sunday Morning
September 23, 1984

Dear Jonathan,

    Fall in New England is something especially marvelous. I wish you and Jack and I were on some trail in the White Mountains this morning!
    I wanted to let you know that I was one of fifteen people accepted for the writing seminar at Radcliffe. Yea!!! This should only enhance my chances for acceptance at Smith. By Christmas I should know if someone in authority believes I have any writing ability.
    If I seemed distracted on our last phone call it was because Tom came into the room in the middle of our conversation. Now that I know how much it really bothers him to hear me talking to another man, I try to consider his feelings. I am sure you understand. Were Gloria in the room, your voice would sound different. More restrained, less friendly.
    The stress of living here has taken its toll. I feel I have aged ten years in this past year. I will be glad when it is all over. I shall start looking for an apartment in Cambridge next week. After Radcliffe, and whatever happens with Smith, if I cannot write I shall move to a warmer climate and clerk in the local grocery store and relate to my fellow man. I plan to reduce the stress of my life and live a much simpler existence. I deserve it.
    I miss you. I wish you felt comfortable seeing me and talking to me, and that the sexual issue had never come between us. We learn by our mistakes.
    Soon, my life shall be better. For now, there is yet a bit more grieving to do.
    Hope all is well with you. It is good to hear that someone's relationship is going better. It gives me hope. Beginning a new business is slow and frustrating but excitement like no other. Call soon.
    Love,

Jasmine

Jasmine Carrietté

October 16, 1984

Dearest Jonathan,

I love talking with you. Thank you for the call. The sharing and intellectual stimulation is on such a high level. I hunger for that rapport, and with you it is as natural as breathing. And NO, *neither* of us should settle for less than that in a primary relationship. Meanwhile, I am happy to have it with you. Jonathan, hold me close in your thoughts, especially until January. I need your love and support.

Jazz

December 15, 1984

Dear Jonathan,

    I am so sorry I missed your call. You know I would return it if that were appropriate, but it is not, of course. Hope all is well with you. I was accepted on almost full scholarship at Smith, so will be on campus beginning January 24th. The Radcliffe Seminars Program also offered me a full scholarship, just to write, so I will be commuting there once a week to work with a professor who thinks I am talented.
    Know you are missed,

Jasmine

The Final Good-bye to Thomas Trout

January 1985, Sudbury, Massachusetts

I sat slumped in the front seat of the car all the way there, sort of on my spine, unable to hold my head up securely by myself. I knew it would be awful, but I had no idea the physical symptoms would be so dramatic. I felt deathly ill. Since seven the night before, I had been vomiting in anticipation and dread. It wasn't going away until this was over.

The drive to Lilly's house was beautiful. Sun sparkled on snow-covered fields of the wealthy west suburban towns we passed, making our way to an appointment I had chosen the year before.

We sat in Lilly's comfortable living room and I looked across out sunny, flower-filled windows to mile after mile of farmland. In the distance was a railroad track, now unused, where an engineer had stopped to call out to Lilly's great-grandfather that Lincoln had been shot. This seventeenth-century farmhouse, which had housed seven generations of Lilly's family, still has the passageways that hid black men and women and children making their way on the Underground Railroad. Across from me in a child's rocker sat a new addition to the toys in the comer. They had been purchased for my benefit, but I never touched them. I wondered if Tom noticed or cared. They sat there, this black Raggedy Ann and Andy, demure, chipper, arms serenely folded, unlike me.

Lilly and I sat in comfortable antique armchairs across from each other in front of a blazing fire, much the way we had sat several times a week for the past year, sipping herbal tea as we talked. Tom was to my right, appearing relaxed and comfortable as always, and belying any attribute of tension, he casually reached for some peanuts Lilly had in a bowl on the glass table in the center of the room. As he reached, he commented, "Well, here we are again."

Lilly, with a pleasant look of peace about her, replied, "Under quite different circumstances."

Still reclining, I said, "I guess I start this off since I requested the meeting."

Lilly asked, "Jazz, are you okay? You don't look your usual self. Do you feel well?"

"I've had vomiting and diarrhea all night, no sleep. It started early in the evening. I thought it was just nerves about facing today, but I'm beginning to believe I have food poisoning. You know me, I think everything is psychological."

"Sometimes you can overdo it. You need to rule out medical reasons first. Are you dehydrated? What did you eat?"

"My friend Diana and I had dinner at a salad bar and I got sick an hour later. I don't feel dehydrated; I just feel tired. I'll watch it."

Cracking peanuts, Tom added, "If I had known you become so docile in front of Lilly, I'd have come here with you more often."

"I'm not docile; I'm ill."

Lilly asked, "Do you want to reschedule this appointment?"

"No. I don't think I'll feel better till this is over."

"Tom, do you understand why Jazz wanted you here today?"

I had a lot of experience at this now, so automatically I turned my body toward him to address him directly. I would have moved the position of my chair to face him, but simply didn't have the energy. "Tom, you've had a major impact on my life. I've spent a lot of time and money and pain in making my decision to leave. I need to know you hear me when I say I love you, and later, once I'm gone, I need an objective, third party to remind me that, yes, I did all I could; I explained my point of view; there was no alternative."

"I know you love me. You've told me that before. I believe you. Why shouldn't you? I've been good to you. I want to restate why I value you and I want to address some painful issues I've never been willing to talk about before."

He was still cracking nuts and eating. Was this the only indication of his feeling nervous? Was this to display his disregard, to indicate nothing of any serious importance was taking place here? What?

"Okay. That's why I'm here, but you already gave me an eighteen-page letter."

"Which you won't read."

Lilly interrupted, "Wait a minute, Jazz. Tom, you haven't read it?"

"I saw no reason to read it when she's going to tell me everything that's in it anyway."

"How does that make you feel, Jazz? To have taken the time and emotional energy to put your feelings and thoughts down on paper and to hear him say he won't read it?"

"It feels very familiar. He's denied me all along. Mostly, I wanted him to have it for those dark, still nights we all have. When he needs to know. He'll read it then, after I'm gone."

"Okay, I'm ready to listen," and he popped another peanut into his mouth.

"First, I want to tell him what he has meant to me."

"Face Tom and address him."

I could feel the tears beginning to come, but this was too important to me and to him. It was an important part of the ritual of letting go. I had to do it, to feel it happening, to know fully, inside my very soul that I was finally, after all these incredible years of pain and passion, going to leave this man. I looked directly at him. "I want to tell you all of the reasons I cherish you and then I want to tell you why I can't stay." Tom made no comment, but began to brush the peanut hulls off his clothes as he braced himself to listen. "I won't dwell on the positive. I've stated it all so often before, but mainly I want to say I've loved the singing. You've got the most beautiful bass voice I've ever heard and I remember the first time I saw you in the trio at church. I've loved the music you've brought into my life and all the pleasure of those hours singing together. I'm especially grateful you enjoy my friends. You're the first extrovert I've ever been involved with, and it's been wonderful to cook together and to entertain friends and know you enjoyed that as much as I do. Singing, sex, and food were our main attractions. You were the first man who ever allowed me any sexual expressiveness in bed and I'm grateful for that freedom. With you, I learned to play, and that delight and wonder I'll always cherish."

"Lots of guys would've done that."

"Tom, are you uncomfortable when she compliments you?"

"She has an incredible imagination."

"And you pretend nothing's happening," I said. "Don't negate reality. You taught me how to run a business. I'd have been successful without you, but your support has made it a joyful experience, and I value your hours of instruction and caring. I appreciate your financial backing at crucial times. I'm glad I've repaid every cent because I didn't realize the emotional bond it became, but you were generous and it wasn't unnoticed. I love you for your patience and tolerance, but most of all for your belief in me. Your innate belief that I could do anything, long before I knew it myself. That, above all, is a most highly prized asset, and the least replaceable, and I love you for it."

"You're not leaving the country, are you?"

"I believe good-byes are always important and necessary," Lilly said. "This is an especially difficult one for both of you, but so crucial to letting go of one another and moving on with your lives."

"She'll be back."

"Do you really think so?"

"She always has."

I listened in disbelief to this exchange between Lilly and Tom.

"In other words, all the work she's done here with me has changed nothing?"

"Nothing. She'll be back."

"When? How long do you think it will take before she's back?"

Tom paused a second to think. "She'll be back within two years."

"I'll wager she won't. Let's agree that two years from this date, which will be January 11, 1987, I'll send a postcard to each of you, wherever you are, and we'll get together again and see who was right."

"Agreed."

"Wonderful."

"Anything else, Jazz, about Tom's positive qualities?"

"Many, but I can't recall everything and it's all in the letter. I just know that when I'm seventy-three and sitting on my front porch rocking, I'll smile with pleasant memories and I'm grateful for them.

"And now for the difficult part."

Tom had finally given up on the nuts, but his attitude had not changed. "Is this going to be serious?"

"It obviously is to me if it brings me to this point. Tom, you've known me long enough to know I would never ask anything of a man sexually that he didn't willingly offer. To me, desire is everything and one cannot legislate for the other. But I want you to know it took me eight months in therapy before I could say to Lilly that you had not kissed me on the lips since our first meeting."

"That's not true."

"It's true. I was not withholding information from her. I couldn't admit it to myself."

"Jazz, kissing and hugging and sitting snuggled together by the fire indicates a kind of relationship I'm unwilling to be involved in. It indicates a future together, a commitment. You know how I feel about that."

"I know we've pretended for years we were in an open relationship when in fact we're together every night."

"Kissing implies something I don't intend to follow up on."

"But making love does not? Holding me all night, often still inside my body, does not? Yes, you're right, kissing is more intimate than hours of sex every day, but denying that to me is demeaning. I couldn't admit it to myself; it was too painful. I never even knew for God's sake.

"Jazz came in here and talked about the wonderful sexual relationship the two of you had. She never mentioned kissing was not a part of it. I'll probably change my therapeutic approach after this and always ask just to be sure."

I turned further in my chair to face Tom more squarely. Reaching for a Kleenex as my eyes again filled with tears, I clutched the arm of the chair. This would be the toughest part. "Tom, although I would never request anything that was not mutually desired, there is one more thing I must ask you because it, too, is why I must leave. Through all the years and all the hours of fellatio, which I loved and wanted and enjoyed as much as you, after hours of oral sex which left blisters on my lips, torn skin inside my mouth, scratches on my face, giving up breath itself to have you deep in my throat, there was never once any indication of the slightest desire on your part to reciprocate with cunnilingus. Before I go, I need to know why."

"It would require an aggressive act on my part. I don't pursue women."

Silence, no one moved. The tears fell to my lap before I could wipe my eyes. "It took me nine years to notice, to allow it into my consciousness, but only a few months to get the courage to ask. Can you imagine the deprivation I came from . . . that I never knew?"

SMITH COLLEGE

January 1985

I walked down Paradise Road toward the pond, and as I started downhill I could see the hummocks rising in the distance with the Chinese footbridge in the foreground just below the waterfall. It was a comforting sight to me. I'd made this walk many times before on my trips to Sage Hall. The island in the middle of the pond was sprinkled with daffodils, and I knew the hill by Wright Hall would be covered with them, too. I remembered the first time I turned that corner at Wright, walking up from Burton, and burst into tears at the sight of those daffodils. That whole first year I had to pinch myself to believe I was really here.

At Tom's house, the temperature inside was never above fifty-five degrees, and often it was lower. Ballpoint pens would not write, ice formed inside the windows. I never felt I had the right to ask him to turn the heat up, and he truly was not cold. Tom never shoveled the walks, and I vividly recall sliding, slipping, stumbling, with all of my equipment, going out to lead sales meetings at night, high heels, no lights, and no sidewalk. I found it incredible a man could live that way and incredible that I chose to live with him.

So it wasn't surprising to me that my first memory of Smith College was warmth, after years of freezing at Tom's. I couldn't believe it when students left their windows open on snowy nights because the dorms were too hot. When I went to the library to do research, I dressed in layers and started peeling off as I entered Neilson: coping with the problems of life was one thing, but coping with the problems of life at five degrees below freezing was even more difficult. The struggle of dealing with a New England winter, the gray bleakness, the snowdrifts, the buried cars made everything seem worse somehow. At Smith it was like fairies had been at work all night, for after a heavy snowfall I stepped out of Franklin King to walks which had not only been plowed but they had been swept and sanded as well.

Tom moved me in my first night at Smith, late January 1985. He seemed to want to know where I was going to be and that I was all right. We were both exhausted, but I insisted on taking him to dinner at Wiggins Tavern before he drove back to Boston. It was a quiet good time. Physical exhaustion left us little energy for verbal repartee. We had said our last good-bye in a three-hour session with Lilly, so this wasn't difficult. I wasn't sure what Tom was really feeling, but that was nothing new. I was elated to be here. We kissed good-bye in the middle of the street in the center of the town that would be my home for the next three years. He kissed me on the lips. My tears were not for me.

During my first few days on campus I had an appointment in the administrative building. Later, I got a note saying, "After you left my office I found a button on my floor. I thought it might be from your raincoat and, if so, it might save you having to sew on all new buttons. Next time you're in College Hall, stop by to see if it's yours." That note would come to signify to me much of what Smith was about—the time and luxury to be gracious. For a woman like myself, from a working-class background, it was significant, this time to be gracious and the luxury to pursue studies of interest. Time for self. I majored in English literature, but I studied things like theatre, too. I had thought theatre a frivolous thing to study, yet I discovered the themes examined were the same which Kierkegaard, Nietzsche, and Otto Rank looked at, only in a less threatening way. I would be able to find answers here.

But there were downsides, there always are. The night before my first exam, I was in the bathroom throwing up from nerves. No matter how much I told myself this was absurd, it did not quell the feeling. I had seen my six-year-old tied in a straight jacket while they searched for a vein in his leg before they decided on surgery. What was an exam by comparison? It didn't help. I ate and drank too much from the stress. After being in my own home for thirty years, I now had to walk sixty feet to the nearest bathroom.

The traditional students teased me about packing up every weekend and checking into the infirmary to be able to sleep. It had been many years since I had teenagers with blasting stereos in my house. I thought of the parents who worried about their daughters out having sex. They needn't have worried; their daughters were out on the lawn screaming. Another negative, I lost my first election for class office and I do not like to lose.

There is a real adjustment to being here. I was so excited about being accepted that I did not realize I was leaving all my friends. I feel like they are two hours away, but they feel like I am gone. They are building new lives for themselves, which do not include me. That is as it should be, but I had not planned on it. I have no sense of where I will be when I get out of here. I do not fit in with faculty. I do not fit in with traditional students. My married friends here go home on weekends. I have no sense of place or identity. I am cut off from my past and do not yet know what my future will be. I am not going back to family or even my home. When you have no identity, you drown. My friend Diana says my leaving Boston has left a great hole in her life. I'm sure she has some anger about that. I do.

Sunday night
February 3, 1985

Dear Jonathan,

It was so good to hear from you. There is so much news to catch up on, but I shall save it until you are able to visit.

I understand Bradley Field in Hartford is about forty minutes away and certainly I could meet you there for a visit, but if you have the time, do plan on a longer stay. It is so beautiful here; I think you will enjoy it. I'll leave that up to you.

I am sending you a copy of my schedule so you will know when I am free.

If we do not make contact soon, I shall write you news of what is happening in my life. I'm glad to hear that all is well with you.

Not sure I understand this, but I do feel so comfortable sharing with you. I always have from the very first meeting.

With much good wishes,

Jazz

Dear Jonathan: I feel compelled to add this and hope I am not complicating the matter. Always, because of the pleasure of talking with you, I have regretted the sex. Not for that act itself, because it gave me so much new information about myself. I learned so much from you; I could not regret that. But because it has strained what could have been a marvelous friendship for me. My invitation to come to Smith is NOT an invitation to have sex with me. It is an invitation to walk and talk and share and see my new environment. I would love to share that with you. I am not ready, not nearly ready for sex with you or anyone. Somehow, you know me; I want things to be perfectly clear. I would love to see you. Consider it. There is always Hartford on a Friday afternoon or evening, and that, too, is fine with me if it seems a more comfortable renewing of our friendship. I'll leave it up to you. There is so much new in my life. If I do not see you soon, I shall write a long letter and fill you in.

Do write. When one is away from friends letters are especially meaningful.

Desire Makes the Difference

Thursday, February 14, 1985
Early morning

Dear Jonathan,

    Thank you so much for calling. It seems we are having a difficult time connecting, doesn't it? I do appreciate your continued effort. Soon, I'm sure the timing shall be right for both of us and indeed we can have that long, face-to-face talk. I relish the thought of finding out all about you. What paths your life has taken this past year and what led you down those paths. I'm anxious, too, to share with you all I've learned about me this year, and hopefully some of it can help you in your own quest.

    The workload at school so far leaves me little time for my own writing, but after this semester that will be different. I'm learning so much, Jonathan, that will help me in my work. I have marvelous, talented professors and I am so excited about what I am doing. I am even taking a theatre course and writing my first play. Definitely not my voice, but a grand stretching exercise. We are studying all major works from every period. It is so wonderful. My fiction class is critiquing major writers such as Chekhov, Faulkner, Joyce, Woolf, etcetera. Truly, I am in love with the teacher. I could sit at his feet and worship. He is one of those venerable, cultured, learned people who has spent his entire life in study and sharing that knowledge with others. He is an absolute joy. They stretch you to the limit here. The reading is insurmountable. The challenge is great. One finally comes to know why and how they earned their reputation. It is good to be a part of it all, to learn and grow and develop fully my craft. They want your success and spare nothing to achieve it. They are very giving, and I am sorry to say I do believe the traditional students are oblivious to the amount of giving on the part of the professors. I am not and count myself truly blessed to be here. Their investment will not be wasted. Funny the roads we take that become, by our choices, our destiny.

    My Radcliffe professor has asked to continue working with me for the next two or three years. I am flattered and indeed shall continue to do so. His feedback is so astute. Hopefully, if all goes well, I want to have a novel ready for print within three years. An agent in New York has already agreed to read my work. Getting read is the hardest part. I'm hoping that by the end of the summer I shall have something to show her for feedback. No matter how good you are, it must be saleable and I will need direction from her about that.

I have a lovely view from my window. I am in a traditional dorm this semester because I came in midterm. I shall have a suite or an apartment, whichever I prefer, in the spring. The food here is wonderful, and it is grand to be relieved of going shopping and cooking. One room with no responsibilities is all I want right now. My goal was to reduce the stress in my life and to have a simpler existence. I've achieved that. With no telephone, my sales unit cannot reach me. I walk at least an hour a day to class and back, which has to be good for my health. The campus is lovely. Finally, those good days I worked so hard for have arrived. I am loving it. I do wish, though, on a Friday night after hours of long hard work—which can be very isolating although hundreds of students surround me—I do wish then, just quietly, I could be held by you briefly the way you held me that first night in Boston. The comfort of being close, I miss. Alas, that is for another time in my life. First things first.

Securely yours,

Jasmine

Desire Makes the Difference

Sunday morning
February 17, 1985

Jonathan,

    Something good happened between us when we met initially, which has nothing to do with the sexual. I do not profess to understand it, but I do look forward to exploring that with you. Do make it happen. Our seeing each other again, I mean. Do come soon to Hartford if even for a short time. I miss you and relish the intellectual, verbal, and emotional bonding I feel with you. Connecting, really connecting with another human being is so rare and wonderful, isn't it?
    Hope all goes well with you. Had an unusual interaction with Blake. Perhaps you can shed some light on it for me. We do struggle to communicate. Maybe there is something I am not seeing, which you have more knowledge of, and I would appreciate your insights when we can talk.
    I am so very sorry I could not get to Hartford that Sunday night. Do you remember the exhaustion of moving? Try me again and with some notice you can be assured I shall make it. Do you get the feeling I am anxious to be in your presence? Shameless of me. Age does carry with it some privilege.
    Your letter was beautiful and I enjoyed it so. Please write more.
    Love,

Jazz

Jasmine Carrietté

April 15, 1985

Dear Jonathan,

    Obviously you are as swamped as I am. The workload here is beyond belief. I am tired now that the semester is ending, but it is a good, marvelous, reinvigorating tired. Know what I mean?
    It has been the best four months of my life. For the first time ever, all of my energies have been fully engaged. I do believe I created crises in my life due to boredom. I remain happy, at peace, feeling fully blessed and for the first time ever, am being nurtured.
    I have rented a place on the ocean for three weeks in Long Beach, North Carolina right after school is out. I shall try to do some writing as well as see my children and walk on the beach. I'm not sure where I will be after that, probably somewhere in Boston working for the summer.
    I don't want to lose touch. Will you please call me before I leave school on May 10th? I need to know all is right in your world before I depart for parts unknown this summer.
    Know I think of you and hope you are well.
    Love,

Jazz

Monday morning
June 17, 1985

Dear Jonathan,

    I arrived home to find your beautiful letter. What a joyful welcome. Two days prior to the receipt of your letter I had the most incredible dream about you.
    I thought of you often as I walked the beach in North Carolina, and it is good to know the memories are not one-sided. Thank you so very much for sharing with me how you reread my letters. It pleasures me to believe I might be a source of continued joy to you as you are to me. Simply the knowing that somewhere in this world there is you. Often my subconscious parades you before me in splendid, conscious, ways. You are a delicious memory, which I cherish.
    The vacation with my children was both good and hard. There was a lot of emotional work I needed to do with them, which, as you so readily know, is difficult but rewarding. I had one week alone that was filled with peace and calm, a wonderful knowing, a certainty. Jonathan, my life is so good now. I would not trade the pain and growth I experienced in 1984 for any amount of money. Daily, I reap the rewards of my efforts and I would not change one thing to go back to my old life.
    My typewriter has been lifted out of the trunk of my car and is currently on the floor of a friend's garage (not the most likely place to compose a letter to you) so that I might get this note off to you. I'll write more later; for now, I wanted to let you know what my plans are.
    From now until July 1st I will be at 617/xxx-xxxx.
    Beginning July 1st I will be at 83 Brattle Street, Apartment 53, Cambridge, MA 02138. I'll send you my phone number as soon as it is installed. I will be at this address for July and August. Then back at school September 1. I'll send you my new address there in my next letter and it will be good for the next two years.

Jasmine Carrietté

    Jonathan, I have a darling, small, sparsely furnished apartment three blocks from Harvard Square. Do plan to come explore with me sometime during July or August.

    I love and miss you.

    More soon,

    Jasmine

July 8, 1985

Dear Jonathan,

　　The last time we talked you told me you had misplaced my first letter to you. Here is a copy just in case you never found it. As you know, I keep a copy of every word I ever put on paper. I have for years. Rereading it more than a year later, I would not change a word. How grateful I am for that experience with you. How perfect was the timing for my life.
　　Summer rushes and I cannot squeeze in all of the things I long to do. A trip to the White Mountains to camp by my favorite lake is a must, but I don't know when. I am finally settled in my own place. It is not too comfortable because there is little furniture, but it does have charm and is in a perfect location.
　　I love and miss you and hope you had a good July 4th holiday. Do write and let me know where you are in your game plan for life.
　　Sincerely yours,

Jasmine

Jasmine Carrietté

July 26, 1985

Ms. Clare Laddman
Ms. Karen Courtfield
Ada Comstock Scholars Program
Smith College
Northampton, Massachusetts 01063

Dear Clare and Karen:

    What a summer! I was unprepared for re-entry. It took two months to understand the adjustments I was making. I have made them now and am enjoying the summer, but still look forward to being back on campus.
    I left school on such a high. I had gone to pick up my theatre project from Mr. Hedwig and received a note which said, "You have done excellent research and creative work. Also the collaborative designs with Mary Ellen Basso are very impressive. The presentation in class was intellectually and emotionally rewarding." Yea for me! You know when I got the "A" from VanderPlas, whom I adore, it completed my joy. For the first time in my life my energies were fully engaged while I was at Smith. It is the most peace I have ever known. For me, Smith was a wonderful time of being nurtured both intellectually and emotionally.
    I have a sparsely furnished, tiny, charming apartment in the Radcliffe Graduate Housing Center three blocks from Harvard Square. It seems I live a fairy-tale existence at fifty-two. I have seen Natalie Douney (she is just across the street) and she wanted to know all about my experience at Smith, which I excitedly shared. She has been helpful and supportive. Clare, she has such admiration for you and what you are doing at Smith. Her comment was, "She works enormous hours and is so dedicated but she is sending women out of that program who will change the world!" She is right, of course, and it makes me glad to hear you receive proper recognition.

Hopefully your summer is going well and you are gaining some much-deserved rest. I miss you all; I miss school; I miss Northampton; I miss the excitement. It will be good to be back. See you soon.

Much love,

Jasmine Carrietté

Jasmine Carrietté

July 29, 1985

Dearest Jonathan,

It was so good to see you again, to walk together and to talk. It was as if I had seen you only yesterday. Conversation comes easily with you, and I like that. I had some new insights about you and your relationships with women, which I will be glad to share when next we meet. I *hear* differently now that I am well, and if my knowledge can help others that makes me glad. Not everyone wants my insight, of course, and I don't offer it to everyone, but I do believe you are on a quest for self and shall share it with you if you so desire.

You shall certainly know me in a most intimate way when you have read the enclosed. I share this much of myself with few people. Truly, I am more vulnerable to you because of it, but I have known your gentleness. It is with trust I offer it and with the belief that shared knowledge offers opportunity for growth.

We had too little time. I hope you do make it back to Boston on an overnight and if you can, do call ahead to let me know so I can get off work early and pick you up. My work # is 647-xxxx ext. xxx. I believe you have my home phone.

Have a great summer. I have already started reading for one of my courses next year. I am hungry for school.

Love you much,

Jazz

No answer necessary. I need to express myself.

August 9, 1985

Dear Jonathan,

At my interview at Radcliffe, the director of the program recommended a book to me that is on all of the reading lists at Harvard. It is *Intimate Strangers: Men and Women Together* by Lillian B. Rubin. My friend Natalie said it is about how two people, a man and a woman, even though perhaps living together, see the same world so differently.

I started reading it today. I cannot express strongly enough to you how much I feel it would answer some of your longing and questioning. I do not agree with your therapist when he says that you should not expect some of the things you do expect from your current relationship, but that is beside the point. All I am writing for is to urge you to purchase and read the book. I have just begun it, but already you are one of the people I felt could profit from it.

DO IT NOW!

Love,

Jazz

Jasmine Carrietté

Wednesday, about 8:00 a.m.
August 21, 1985

For one of the few times in my life I feel rather speechless. I am sitting in Brinkley's at the Ramada Inn by Logan Airport having a quiet, contemplative, leisurely breakfast.

Last night I spent the night with Jonathan. He arrived at 10:00 p.m. and left at 8:00 a.m. We talked much of the night. I cannot describe the closeness I feel to him. I share an intimacy with Jonathan, which I share with only one other: Glenn Bowman. Glenn, through the years of letter writing and a long-ago personal history; Jonathan, of course, more recently. It is not insignificant, I think, that both are articulate; not only verbally in their ability to express their feelings, but in writing as well. I have no research statistics at hand, but I wonder if there is not a correlation in an ability to put pen to paper and an ability to be in touch with one's emotional side. Certainly it is a prerequisite in sharing who we are with others, and *that* beyond any doubt is what I seek in a relationship.

This morning as I sit and look at the travelers around me, it recalls a world I left five years ago. My world at Smith is so different. I notice a difference in the travelers, too. There are more women traveling on company business. Interesting, though, that they are invariably traveling with men. The company has been forced into a posture of seeming acceptance but does not yet trust a woman to be competent to do it alone.

I have been sitting here trying to be in touch with exactly what it is I am feeling, and to not only know for sure, but to be able to express it. It finally came to me what I could not express or put to words all night: I am no longer *tyrannized* by sex. It is a first. A new thing in my life. I made the decision about what I wanted to do last night with Jonathan. That is a first! Jonathan had no part in my decision (nor was I responding to the bonds of my heritage). That is, I felt no pressure from Jonathan either way. In fact, quite the opposite. I felt a true concern on his part that I do nothing to damage myself, because he understands so accurately where I am, what I am feeling, what I need and seek. He also knows and has stated accurately he cannot give me that right now, so I felt no pressure from him but rather support for whatever decision I might make.

I felt equal support for both, although I must state, too, I also felt desired. I knew as well that had my decision been not to make love with him, he too felt my desire for him. I believe we had both felt the intimacy, a closeness, not only intellectually and emotionally but physically as well: a like response, if you will, to physically touching or being touched. He is always "so there" with me physically. There is no void, no blank spaces in the energy. For every movement, no matter how delicate, there is a like response. He is so *with* me, so *there*, so connected in mind, body, and spirit. It is unique. We touch in similar ways. Never has the physical been so concrete. One can count on a response from Jonathan, expect it. So often in touching, even with a good lover, there are voids, things left undone one would have liked completed. Jonathan keeps his hands so closely on my genital pulse. He knows when I am climaxing, no guessing—as with some men—and thus knowing, provides exactly what I need to complete a really hard orgasm. But that does not really explain it either, for it is there from the first contact. The touching *gives* as much to Jonathan as it gets for him. I know. I can tell because I am the same way and one can recognize it in another. I know from Glenn's letters, too, although we have never had sexual intercourse, he is the same way. They are the only two men I have ever met who are like this. Is this, too, this ability to touch this way, also connected to their ability to express feelings both verbally and in writing? I wonder. Good guidelines and indications certainly. I was not wrong to admire a man of letters.

I have not begun to describe last night yet, my feelings about it, my thought processes in coming to the decision that Jonathan and I could have sex without changing our relationship in any negative way, but unfortunately I, too, am of the world and must stop now to go to work. Hopefully, when I can be alone again, I will not have lost all of what I am now feeling and will be able to put it into words. Suffice it for now to say I feel wonderful, not only physically (who wouldn't after last night) but mentally and emotionally as well. I am at peace.

Thank you, Lilly and Jonathan, for walking this path with me.

Jasmine Carrietté

August 26, 1985

My dear friend,

You have a profound effect on me, you always have. The enclosed will show you how I am thinking. More will follow. Being held and touched after such a long time is a story within itself, but being held and touched by you is something of significance I want to be able to write about. As I said before: there is a difference.

I leave for school on Saturday and will be so happy to be going back.

You are very much with me and I have such strong feelings I want to express; hopefully, soon there will be time for doing that.

Thank you for everything. You are such a dear and wonderful friend.

I love you,

Jazz

April 6, 1986

Dearest Jonathan,

How I wish that all of the knowledge I've gained through my pain could miraculously be imparted to you. How grand that would be, if we could shield those we love from making similar mistakes. Alas, it can't be done. These many months of silence between us have been a gulf, a void, across which I could not reach to touch or ease your pain. I knew it was there, sensed something was wrong. It was unlike you not to have written. Some paths we have to walk alone. I'm sorry. Why could you not reach out to friends for support? It seems there are many in your life who would offer comfort.

I've thought of you much lately. If I remember correctly, Gloria was moving April 1st. I love you and I know the pain of separation is grievous. Therefore, I attempt to project some aura of protection to surround you and support and comfort you during these days and weeks. If loving thoughts had the power to heal, you would be well by now, my love. Alas, they cannot, but hopefully it helps to know your friends are remembering you.

My life is so oneness directed. It used to be sex. Now it is school. Regardless, no matter which it may be, I have no balance in my life and do need that. I feel I am beginning to be in a place where I would enjoy relating to some significant "other" again. But as you are so well aware, relationships take so much time and energy, and I have little of that to spare right now. It is not healthy to do only one thing. Balance is important.

Finally, one must have a break. I have worked on papers for school until I am exhausted. Do you remember how tired you get toward the end of the semester? Four more weeks and this semester will be over. Thank God. It has been hard. In thirteen weeks, I've had twenty-nine papers. Enough already. I'll write my proposal about my work for the next two years as soon as school is out. Once it is accepted, I am pretty much on my own. That, hopefully, will ultimately produce a book in print and I am anxious to start the work. I have not written since my arrival here.

I've enclosed my schedule for the summer. Please keep it so you will know where I am. Jonathan, if you will note I am free in Northampton May 9-28. Can you plan to visit me at some point during that time? School will be closed, so we would not have the fun of attending various functions, but you could see the campus. I have a large, comfortable apartment and I live alone. I'd like a few days to get to know you better. The last time I had sex, it was with you. The next time I have sex, I'd like it to be with you. I have had a horrible semester. I need to be held and touched. I want to touch. I'd like to share comfort and excitement with you. If you can, will you come? I have not wanted to be sexually involved with anyone. I do with you. The proposal may be totally out of keeping with your mood and what you are facing right now, and if it is, I understand and apologize for being so indelicate as to make such a proposal when you are in the midst of adjusting to the loss of someone you love. However, you cannot know what I am feeling unless I tell you. I don't expect you to be able to read my mind. If I am being really gauche and insensitive in the middle of all your pain, you have my sincerest apology.

With my invitation goes also my ability to hear you say it is not an appropriate response on your part right now. I have the right to ask. You certainly have the right to refuse. Regardless, even if it is not something you can or are inclined to respond to right now, I have always had the feeling, since I first met you, that at some point in time we would have an opportunity to know one another better. I can wait. You're worth waiting for.

I recall kneeling at your feet near the foot of the bed with your lovely organ in my mouth. I recall reaching up your long legs to grasp your buttocks in my hands, then moving them searchingly up your tall, slim body to feel your smooth, flat stomach, then back to carefully guide the movements of your phallus in my mouth. I recall the touch of your hands on my head and your comments to me about how it made you feel. I recall asking you to lie back on the bed so I might be more aggressive. You are so tall; I cannot get you in my throat in that position—your phallus pointing straight up and my throat curving down—and wanting more, and I, too, feeling the excitement and desire building within me sought deeper penetration and once you were on the bed, then I, kneeling beside you, were free to control my movement and the depth of penetration at will; but, alas, I'm out of practice and the head of your phallus so large and the need to be completely relaxed required to allow the gag reflex to become inoperative. Our relationship is new and I, so inexperienced with you, am unable, without more leisure time together, to culminate the quintessential act, for me, of feeling you all the way down my throat. To stop the gag reflex I must hold my breath but cannot when I am this excited. Perhaps I can calm down . . . with more time together. Our lack of experience with one another limits me. Will I hurt you? How sensitive are you to pain? It must be a mutual desire. My love of experimenting must be shared, but we have not talked enough for me to know if you delight as I do in this experience.

My sexual feelings and fantasies about you, my differences since my wellness, my meeting you at the point of change in my life, all spur me on to seek greater knowledge of you, physically, intellectually, and emotionally.

How I would love days to explore your body. Time. It is what I need to know you, especially geographically, the landmarks of your body. Time is what I want to experiment, to explore, and to be satiated. To rest and then discover again your boundaries. And mine. The physical horizons we might share are as yet untouched. Good sex is enhanced by communication. With the verbal rapport we have, we have a head start. We've only had sex late at night after you've worked all day and with little time to get reacquainted. Can you imagine what a weekend would bring?

Be well, know I hold you close in my thoughts, as do others I am sure. You are such a fine young man. I know well the pain of separation from someone you love. I suffered physical pain; the anguish was so great. Know it passes. Time and growth change the pattern of your life. My life is immensely better. You know that. Hugs and kisses until I see you.

Love,

Jazz

Jasmine Carrietté

November 1, 1986
4:30 a.m. (been up all night)

Dear Jonathan,

    Always, it pleases me to talk to you, and no matter the months between conversations, it seems like yesterday since we spoke. From the very beginning I felt easy with you, on the same wavelength, and although I don't believe in reincarnation, I do feel otherworldly about my relationship with you. You are special. And always after a conversation with you, I feel I have been physically touched and it is good.

    I've been up all night just savoring being alive and in this world, and the wonderful opportunity I have of being able to do exactly as I please. I don't have cancer—Yea! For the last two years I have had a greater sense of peace than at any time in my life. You come to a real sense of your aloneness at this age. You deal with it, come to terms, have some sadness about it, accept it, and then nothing looks as frightening ever again. It is truly a good place to be. I love you and miss you and am glad you are well. I'm so sorry I never knew about your injury, but I'm glad you are healed.

    Love,

Jazz

Desire Makes the Difference

November 6, 1986

Dear Jonathan,

I heard something in your voice last night I've never heard. It took much of the morning for me to figure it out. There is an energy in your voice that was never there before. It appears your decision about business has freed you in some way—as though all the energy it took to sit on the fence, balancing, is now active.

Isn't it amazing how we continually give all our power away and how absolutely great and energized we feel when we take it back? I just wanted you to know it was obvious.

Much love,

Jazz

Jasmine Carrietté

Sunday
December 7, 1986
Journal

    I just came from vespers on the Smith campus. There was a hundred-voice choir, a fifty-piece orchestra, handbell ringing, several other choirs in the balcony, many unusual instruments, candles, a huge unadorned Christmas tree, poinsettias, laurel wreaths several hundred feet long, and an organ.
    Wonderful, it was absolutely wonderful. There was a special soloist and another choir singing from the rear of the auditorium. I sat there alone. I sat and cried for the gift of my life and for how I live it now, for Smith and all it means to me. I came here two years ago. I am a different person. Thank God. Thank Lilly. Thank me. Thank my mom and dad for the brains I inherited and the courage I have so that I had the nerve to fight and to try. I made it. This is the most wonderful Christmas of my life. I am happy. I am alone but not lonely. It is a wonderful Christmas and a happy New Year.

January 27, 1987

Dear Jonathan,

    In the last few days I have started and stopped and begun and torn up numerous letters to you. None of them conveyed what it is I feel. For someone normally so verbal, there were no words. Basically, what I was trying to express is how glad I am that you are coming to see me. For a long time now I have wanted to share with you the space in which I live and work and study. This is such a peaceful, good time in my life. I love it here, and since I love you, a natural extension of that is wanting you to be acquainted with my surroundings. Smith has nurtured me so. This is a glorious place to me, these years precious.

    I was beginning to feel that because of your busy schedule, your need to get a new business up and running, your working out of your long relationship with Gloria, and the time demands all of these things make on you, that somehow I would have left Smith and never been able to share it with you. I am thrilled you are planning to come in February. Simply to touch your hand as we talk. I remember with excitement your long, sensuous, graceful hands—they set my mind ablaze. The intimacy I feel when we are together, simply being in your arms and sharing, means so much to me. This—you and me—our relationship—is different, but sharing is important to me and never changes.

    Jasmine

Jasmine Carrietté

February 18, 1987

Dear Jonathan,

February has come and nearly gone with not one word about your trip to Smith. Please do not despair or fret about it. It is not the best time to see the campus. We are covered by several feet of snow and it is freezing. I did not want my recent letter about sharing to make you feel pressured. It should not. I have to say what I believe, but I think you know me well enough by now to realize I expect you to take care of yourself in our friendship and to do what you need to survive. Surviving, simply surviving, takes all our energies some days, doesn't it?

Know you are loved and cherished in my memory, and when the time is right we can spend some days together. I am just glad you want to make the effort to come to Smith before I leave.

My health has been just awful lately. Doctors drive me nuts and I am so impatient for remedies to be effective. Hopefully, this next month should find much improvement, and boy I am ready for that. One of the symptoms is sleep deprivation and it finally takes such an unpleasant toll on my ability to work productively.

Have you heard from Blake? I have called him twice, several weeks apart, and sent him a card. No response. That is unlike him. Perhaps he is just busy or madly in love, but he has always been really good about keeping in touch. I hope he is okay emotionally.

Hope your business goals are clearly defined. Did you affirm them to someone? If you've ever studied values clarification, it's one of the signs they're real goals, goals of importance to you.

Love you,

Jasmine

March 8, 1987
Late Sunday Afternoon

Dear Jonathan,

This has been the most beautiful weekend. I wish you had been here to spend it with me. The flower show is something special every year, and the singing groups on Saturday night were fun as usual. The sun is out and it is 70 degrees. I took many long walks and a long drive down back-country roads and thought of you.

The desire to be with you was so unusually strong this weekend. In three years, I have been almost totally celibate. I had sex with you two or three times, and once with Blake. Other than that, I have chosen to be alone. I have felt happy and peaceful. My work comes first.

I feel healthy and strong enough now to begin reincorporating the physical part of my life into the spiritual and emotional and intellectual, and quite naturally my thoughts turn to you. You were the last person I had sex with, and you are the only person I have ever had sex with who allowed me to receive so completely. You know how special I feel about you because of that, and well, this weekend, today, I just wish I could lie by your side, in your arms, and be held. The comfort, the incredible comfort of that with someone I value and who evidences a valuing of me, is so important right now to me.

I think you will be sorry if you don't have longer to stay because it is so pretty here and there is so much to see and do, but regardless, come when you can. Know you are held in my thoughts and I wish for you a good week of well-being.

Sincerely yours,

Jasmine

Jasmine Carrietté

March 24, 1987

Dearest Jonathan,

    Outwardly, you project a refined elegance that is beautiful to watch. On my bedroom floor you evidenced an earthiness that touched some equally responsive primitive core in me. It was wonderful.
    Thank you.

Jazz

March 31, 1987 (*never sent—just thinking out loud*)

My dearest Jonathan,

    There is a heavy, steady, winter rain this morning. It will be with us all day. Socked in—is that the expression? And I am snuggled down emotionally inside myself with feelings and thoughts of you. Sharing, simply walking on campus or downtown, a cup of coffee, looking over the ridge at Amherst. All of that holds such meaning after three years of aloneness. It was so special and I'm glad I waited to share it with you. Jonathan, sex is so special with you. I love the way you touch. I can still hear your voice describing the response my body has to your arousal. It was beautiful to hear and still remains even now a turn-on to me when I recall it.

    I must get back to work. Rain cannot delay my schedule. I have a task to complete, but I just wanted to take a side trip for a few minutes to recall this past week with you. Touching was so good after such a long time. Being with you nourished my soul. Simply being by your side. Sharing the same space. Something happens to the molecules in my brain when you are in my environment.

    Jasmine

April 1, 1987

My dear man,

What is it you have done to me? After a three-year abstinence, being "turned on" again seems rather like being in hell. God, what beautiful memories of you have danced in my head this day. Incredible. You are an overwhelming lover. I have had some small amount of guilt. Did you feel as though you were sexually abused? I hope not. You are so lovely to touch and, Jonathan, never have I been so wet as when you put your hands on me. When you articulated the changes you felt in my body as I responded to your touch, I found that such a turn-on. It is true. Your description was so accurate. I can feel the swelling as the labia part to receive you. I do respond so to you, my love. I love your hands on and in me.

Enough, I am driving myself crazy. I wish so much that you were closer. A six-hour visit to Hartford would do me just fine right now!

Jazz

April 2, 1987

Dear Jonathan,

    I'm sane again today, great. Hormones? Memories? What havoc they play with our lives. Thank heavens I'm better. I had a meeting this morning with my reader from Academic Development and am going to Boston tonight to take Thomas Trout to a Celtics game. The tickets were a corporate gift from my friend Diana. It should be fun.
    I'm excited about my work. The more I talk to women, the more I know I have something of value to share. My freedom of expression, I hope, can aid them in being free. Admitting what we feel, that is the beginning of awareness, and only then, from that place, can we make accurate choices. What I am doing is so hard. The feeling it may be worthwhile is all that keeps me going some days.
    Your visit came at such a crucial time. It was a turning point for me. I'm sorry if I appeared more insecure and needy than usual. I did not feel that way by the time you left. Thank you. Somehow the validation of talking, walking, being touched, being held, sharing with a male who evidences some valuing of me, came into play somewhere in there and was a major event.

Jasmine

Jasmine Carrietté

April 4, 1987

Dear Jonathan,

The Celtics played Detroit. Isiah Thomas was something else to watch. Wow! What a hustler. Detroit far outplayed the Celtics and should have won. Thomas put the game into overtime with only five seconds of play left. A real thriller.

Thomas Trout asked me to sleep with him that night. That is not an easy thing for him to do and it is a first. I said, "Sure, if you kiss me all night on the lips, give ME an oral and spend the next six holidays with me." He said, "We'll talk about it in the morning." I said, "I'll sleep upstairs until in the morning." In his subtle, quiet way, he never gives up. It would be death for me and is not something I would ever consider. How sad for two people who care so much for one another. I told him you wanted to meet him. Maybe we can arrange something in Boston sometime. I go there often, lately every week.

I wanted to tell you what a wonderful visit I had with Blake. It felt really good to catch up on where he is in his life. I'm happy with what I see. He is growing. He was really helpful with my workout. I'm doing twenty minutes on the bicycle, at your suggestion, and he suggested two repetitions on the machines, which gives me a much more vigorous workout. I feel great. Thank you both. Of course, I would always like to end my workout as I did with you, but what the hell, you can't always have everything the way you want it, right?

Jazz

April 5, 1987

Dear Jonathan,

Sunday night—after two days of rain I still feel great.

I have listened to your tape once and made notes. I am listening to it again and typing out my response for you. It will take a good deal of time, so I may send it to you piecemeal. This is my first few minutes' reaction (on the next page). I have such strong feelings about the things I heard you saying on the tape and am anxious to share them with you, but am pressed for time with school ending in four weeks. Suffice it to say for now, the major reaction is how much you keep to yourself. No, Jonathan, people cannot read your mind and you should not expect them to. I have so much I want to say about implied and implicit relationships. I may end up sending you a tape later—after school is out. I did photocopy the pictures of Glenn Bowman. Look at his face, his eyes—I just got the last picture yesterday. It breaks my heart to see the grief in his eyes. Notice, too, the Oxford shirt.

It is late and I am getting tired. I'll get this off to you tomorrow if possible. I am concerned about you—not in any serious way but just the fact that NO ONE would ever believe you could ever be depressed. You are so good-looking, so personable, so tender, so sensitive—anyone would believe you had all good things coming to you, were happy and content and at peace. Your tape tells me otherwise. For now, I'll check in on you. Know I love you. I hope you have a good week—my days have certainly been more peaceful since your visit. I love you and hold you close.

Soon,

Jazz

My response to your tape:
Seeker of truth—Yes, I would agree that accurately describes you.
Few men are on a quest. You are one of them—and yes, it includes the spiritual. I am only now beginning to realize how much. It takes

a while to see that about you. I do believe people respond so to the physical beauty of you. They miss the spiritual, the much-higher-than-average sensitivity. Absolutely agree, that is why you and I could talk immediately upon meeting. It is what makes you such a good lover. It is what makes you so responsive to others' needs.

Because I am around you so little, I do not actually observe you with negative people where you hurt yourself because of your sensitivity. But I have always wondered why you do not spend more time with people who make you feel positive. Your relationship to Gloria seems to drag you down and yet you are drawn to her. You seem, in fact, to be waiting for her to return and take up where she left off. By your indecision you will be acted upon rather than act. This, after knowing full well the negative aspects of the relationship. So although I don't see you do it, yes, I hear that you do.

You asked your therapist how you could recognize this, when your sensitivity is damaging you by being with negative people. The way I recognize it is, I ask myself, "Do I feel better or worse about myself after spending time with that person?" The answer is always crystal clear. You do need to learn to recognize when people are hurting your own self-esteem. It is always so subtle. Self-esteem is fragile and needs good caretaking. Your therapist said there is a way of recognizing it before it happens. I'm not sure I agree with that, but yes, you can recognize certain people where it always happens when you are around them, and those folks you learn to stay away from. (I'm not talking about Gloria.) I don't know your friends.

Referring to the fact your therapist recommended you should observe more, I think you back away and just observe too much already. She said you should observe. I think you need to speak up and express your pain, how that person is making you feel, or remove yourself from their presence. You turn inward too much already. You've observed enough. I think you need to speak more about what you are experiencing; pain, hurt, whatever.

Absolutely—you do have an easygoing way about you that makes people feel relaxed. After listening to the tape, I learned more about you than in all of our personal encounters. I'm beginning to wonder if there is not a very tightly coiled spring in there, ready to snap. There is a look about you (and I am sure it is partly supplied by some inner spiritual peace, but it is supplied, too, by your elegant appearance) which inspires a still confidence. Your quietness denotes one thing. I'm sensing now another. Oh my God, Jonathan, do speak. There are many who will love you and feel even closer to you. Your looks separate you, place you apart. No wonder you feel isolated and alone.

I'm going to try to photocopy some pictures and send them along with this note. Watch the changes over the years from 1964 to 1987. Look at the haunted, spiritual pain in this man's eyes. Reach out. Appearance was always so important to this man. You've said it is to you. To me, I'd rather risk rejection of the real me than acceptance of the false.

Jasmine Carrietté

May 5, 1987

Dear Jonathan,

God I love you.

I took the liberty of showing your letter to a friend whose opinion I value. She said, "Never in all of literature have I ever seen a man write to a woman like that. It is the most beautiful letter from a man that I have ever read. It is how women want to be spoken to." Yes, that is the key. It is how women want to be spoken to. Unfortunately, they never are. Thank you, Jonathan, for your love and your ability to express it. We do have a very special relationship. Yes, your sensitivity calls for someone special. One of the reasons I have been rather down the last few weeks concerns relationships and my seemingly inexplicable inability to relate—much what you are feeling.

Lilly says, because of my intelligence and my verbal ability, my fearlessness about rushing in and discussing issues which others feel are off limits, will call for a man equally intelligent, articulate, and especially courageous. Courage, yes, I have plenty of that, too. I never thought of it as courageous to take the steps I've taken. I've always seen myself as a risk taker but never a gambler, and there is a big difference. I do take risks, but I weigh the odds before I begin and know I have a better than average chance (given my tenacity) to succeed. Most men, even bright men, want comfort, peace in their lives, to be settled, content with a good little wife who will come home from work every day and take care of them. Essentially, to still be able to nurse at the breast. You know I'll never provide that. Love, affection, attention, of course (and I believe to a degree they would get nowhere else), but I'll never be settled and not growing, going on to the next adventure to seek what it is I don't yet know. Peace, yes, but it is an inner peace; not the comfort of acquiring material goods. Those don't bring peace. Ask Thomas (and I hate to shop!).

What I started out to prove before I got sidetracked is to say that I understand now that Lilly is right. It is not me who cannot relate.

Desire Makes the Difference

I require a different quality of person. It is not my fault that men my age are more cautious and, although attracted greatly to me, are a little terrified also. So be it. I can wait for that one person who can share on my level. What I am saying is that any man who can write the letter you wrote to me has a special set of problems in finding a woman who can relate to you. You've got the same problem I have, only reversed due to gender and age. It is not an easy problem to solve, but Jonathan, I am here to tell you that from this perspective—this perspective of more years on this earth than you have—never, not once, in my entire life have I ever regretted that I feel things to the degree and depth that I do. Yes, I feel pain to a greater degree, but I also feel joy and sensuality and happiness, and get to see that world. I have a vision that others never have because they are closed to it and afraid to look. Keeping one's self numb, to get through the pain of living, blocks out the joy as well. Yes, you'll have a tougher time finding someone to relate to because of your ability to empathize, because you have a vision they don't share. But don't ever trade the gift. Cherish it, nourish it, value it as you would any precious gift. Even alone, we enjoy more than many people who are able to share with someone else.

Another issue: I've been alone now for a little over three years. Now, only now, at fifty-four, after aloneness and all the therapy I've had, am I able to contemplate for the first time in my life an adult, equal relationship. If you are alone for a long while, don't fret about it, hug it to you, grow, do the things you want to do, be selfish, cherish yourself and you will know when you are ready to seek a partner (and your ability to choose the right person will be in place, effective, to enable you not to make destructive choices anymore). I am here to tell you one or two dates, one short note, I know. I don't have to spin it out to eight years as I did with Thomas Trout. It's wonderful. The confidence I feel about knowing is wonderful. Not that they are bad people, but I know they're not for me. There is a sureness about my choosing now that was never there before. It is grand.

Aloneness can be terrifying. Coupling provides our only comfort in our endeavor to push back the specter of the grave, that ultimate time of being alone when no one can reach us. It takes a special person to encounter that prospect before our time arrives to do so. Not being part of a couple, by choice, forces us to confront death—the ultimate aloneness. Few people have the courage to do it. Fear has never held me captive—nor does it you.

Jazz

Sometime the last week of September 1987

My dear Jonathan,

    I awoke this morning to a dream of you and decided to share it. I woke as I reached for you. You were settling over me. Your long body extended as you reached and lowered yourself. At the same time, stretching, hovering above me, you bent your head to kiss my shoulder, and as you did, sensing your body over me, I awakened and reached to trace the long line of your torso with my fingers, down your left side to settle on your narrow hip. I sensed your preparation to enter me, and placing my other hand on your other hip I guided you to sit gently on my chest. With most of the weight on your knees, you rest lightly there and are free to place your hands anywhere on me, and I, I sense such power in you as I reach up to place my hands first on your chest. Your beautiful organ rests comfortably below my chin, brushing my face upon occasion, and I move your shoulders back away from me so I can look up at you. Visually, you please me. I want you just to be there and to let me enjoy you. I reach with both my hands to lift your organ to my face, to make it more accessible to me. I take this most beautiful, incredible, pleasure-giving instrument in my hands, and with such love and such awe at the wonderful feeling it inspires and elicits, I close my eyes to enable me to feel every nuance it brings to my brain—the length, the width, the man it is attached to, and who he is and what he stands for, predominantly it is his sensitivity which makes this organ, out of all others, so attractive to me. Cupping my long fingers vertically down both sides, I attempt to contain it in my hands. I cannot, but I do expose all the sensory nerve receptors in my fingertips to the feel of your phallus. Caressing it, loving it, losing myself in the incredible, beautiful feel of it, I am reluctant to let it go.

    Gradually, I lift your phallus to my face and rub it, lay it, press it, roll it against my face with my hand. I want you so. You are so pleasing to me. I want to reach up once again and touch your long slim body. Your height is such a physical turn-on for me. I want to touch you; I know you are there but I cannot let this gorgeous instrument go. I have felt such sensory deprivation these last few years and I do not for a minute want to let you out of my hands. I continue to feel you against my face. It is wonderful, feeling the different and varying textures of skin on your penis, like velvet.

Reversing my hands now, placing my thumbs against the base of your prick and extending my fingers down either side, I direct the head of it nearer my mouth. Turning my hands now to hold the shaft, with my thumb underneath the base of the glans, I guide the head of your penis with all its warmth, and feeling the engorgement of blood, almost as though this begins some ritual sacrifice, I open my mouth to receive you, but instead reach with my tongue to welcome you into my body. My God, you are so warm and so firm, yet your rigid flesh yields to my touch. You enter across my lips, and with my tongue I can feel absolutely every pulse, every beat, every quivering movement of your body extended into this, its most sensitive organ. I feel you, all of you within this instrument. It is the very closest I can get to you. You are contained within me now in a way vaginal intromission never quite contains you. My tongue against your phallus senses every heartbeat. I can caress you here, express myself with you here, in a way nothing else allows me. Just as your hand on my clitoris allows you to monitor my sexual pulse, my tongue in one long stroke up the shaft of your penis flips and lifts and curls and circles, and then my mouth and lips, enclosing the head of your phallus, allows your glans to burst into my mouth like a ripe, swollen plum, dripping moisture, filling it and allowing me to know exactly where you are sexually, minutely, in the most definitive way possible.

I am lost, hopelessly lost. I will and can and do spend hours here, as long as you will let me. I am obsessed. I love, simply love, having your prick in my mouth. It pleases me so. Something Lilly and I have never completely pieced together continues to make me so obsessed with fellatio. I hope a part of that never gets healed so I will never lose the incredible joy I find in the practice of it with you. My genital area long ago has swelled, filled with blood. Scarlet now, the lips have swollen and parted, and I did not have to wait to feel your long slender hands on me. You offer me some small sense of control. You calm me. At times, holding you in my mouth, I feel like I will leave this planet. Your hands on me bring me back to earth. I must let go emotionally but be grounded to build to the orgasm you are preparing for me. I reach it. I reach it so easily with you. Never any desire or hesitation to hold back anything. I know I am safe. My mouth is dry now from hyperventilation, and I've had to take you out for a moment to recover from my own orgasm. Slowly, softly, you bring me down, never removing your hand from me, you let me return to this world in my own good time. Stillness, you do not move, you simply hold me and wait. Briefly, I have been away. But now, sensing my readiness, you move your hands over me once again and I am free to go back to you, and holding your phallus in my hands I return you once more to my mouth. You move up and over me, onto your hands, which allows you deeper penetration. I move my hands onto your hips and your rigid member has a life of its own, moving in and out of my mouth, across and past my lips, teasing me by withdrawing almost completely and then plunging, but not too deeply, not deep enough to hurt me. The excitement, the friction builds until I want to scream, but any sound is muffled. My mouth is full. I want you. God I want you. I try to push you off me but you do not let me move at first. You know what I want, but you know as well how much that desire increases my tempo. If we are to play for hours I cannot do it yet. But I want you. I want you deeper than this. I want so badly to feel you in my throat. I push you off me, onto your back. You lie there, unwilling to give in so quickly, but knowing I will allow no less. Knowing it gives me my greatest pleasure, and unwilling to prolong any longer the exquisite ecstasy of it, you ask about pleasuring me more first, and I explain this is the quintessential pleasure for me. I move my left arm up your long torso, wordlessly signaling you to lie back and just enjoy. Momentarily you hesitate. I can see you deciding silently whether to give me my way, whether to allow me my own joy, or whether this is one of those times you will heighten my pleasure by forcing me to accept pleasure.

You let me have my way. It is always so wonderful that I never know for sure. I cannot count ahead of time on being sure which it will be. You are such fun. You are the only man I trust to put his head between my legs. It makes me feel more vulnerable than anything else I have ever done. I'll let you there, forever. I would now if you made me. But

I smile and am glad you're letting me have my way with you. Not yet sure you're completely mine—the way I desire to have you—I briefly leave my left hand on your chest to be certain you are staying where I put you. Then I gently bring my hands to meet as I gather your testicles within them, and kneeling by your side I bury my face in these glorious, delicate, sensitive, mercurial, lovely gifts. I gently roll them between my fingers. I lick them. I feel their texture in my mouth. God, they are wonderful. I think they are toys made especially for me. I begin to lick the anterior side of your phallus. It is hard, rigid, standing so erect it faces back toward you, and I, kneeling over you, have full and total control. What I wanted from the very beginning.

May 1988
Journal

And now it is time to go. I know what it is that is so important about this place. I spent last summer at Cambridge in England studying Shakespeare. There was something of grave importance going on in one of my courses, and I went to the director of the program to inform him. He said, "Surely you must be mistaken." I realized that was the first time anyone had spoken to me like that since I arrived at Smith. What happens that is of such importance at Smith is that no one, absolutely no one, ever questions our integrity. First and foremost, we are believed. We are listened to, whether it be in the classroom or with some administrator. Never does anyone question that we have a right to speak or should be heard. Never does anyone question our motivation. First, our voice is honored. Should investigation prove we might be in error, someone comes back to us and says, "Did you ever think of it this way," or, "could such-and-such possibly be an explanation," or, "Our research shows . . ." But never is our word doubted. There is something that takes place internally after being validated in this way. We, as women, come to believe in our right to be listened to, to be heard. Had I been at Smith when I was eighteen, how different my life would have been. I look at these young women and realize that somehow, innately, they know, that later they are going to need these years apart that Smith provides for them. I am so grateful for the women who have kept Smith apart and separate all these years so that when I needed the isolation and separateness, it was here for me.

The Ada Comstock Scholars Program, which consists of nontraditional students over the age of twenty-three, have a dinner given for them at graduation. We were each asked to say a few words. I spoke first and I made it brief.

"Several years ago my sister, Jessica, said to me, 'Jazz, you'd be amazed at what you could accomplish if you spent less time in the bed with Thomas Trout.' I quite literally had to get out of the bed with Tom to come to Smith College. For the past three years I've spent a great deal of time in bed with Shakespeare and Chaucer, Proust and

Faulkner. They've been the most enduring, sustaining, and enriching relationships with men that I have ever had. This is the first spring I did not cry when I saw the daffodils by Wright Hall. No longer do I feel like the sprightly flower being bounced around by the wind. But rather, I've come to feel more like the bulb, firmly grounded, with all the nutrients I need to feed myself."

EPILOGUE

Dad gave me an invaluable gift that has helped me get through life. He taught me it was okay to be different. He taught me it was okay to question authority. And he taught me, as I would desperately need to know later in the business world, that it was okay to respond to the statement, "We have always done it this way." He was eccentric. Even as a child, you could not miss that fact. Pop, as the grandchildren would later call him, gave no credence to what others might think. He never charged anything in his life, not a car, not land, and not a home. He paid cash, so he felt like he owed no one—thus he owed no one an explanation. Little did I know how much this one trait would save me in the end. The end of me, that is. When I came to the end of life, I had no regrets. I never said, "What if?" I never said, "Only if." I had risked. I had been vulnerable. I had questioned. I had tried. There is no greater gift, I think, than love.

ACKNOWLEDGMENTS

I have many to acknowledge for this publication. First, there is Edgar F. White, IV (Ted), who in November of 2009 quite literally saved my life on two occasions, with me fighting him all the way. God bless you, Ted, for pulling me through.

Christopher Snyder, who, with no recompense, a recent job promotion with added responsibilities, and a new love in his life, took his time to transform a 27-plus-year-old manuscript using optical character recognition in order for it to be used in today's technology. Without him this book would have never been published. In addition, he kept me laughing and comforted with great hugs. I love him. Who wouldn't?

Timothy A. Parvin, whom I met just as I was accepted, as one of 15, for the Radcliffe Seminars Program, nurtured me all the way to graduation at Smith. However, he has never let me forget my obligation to write. In small, loving ways, over 31 years he has nudged me to fulfill my gift. Never rude, always gentle—but relentless: he beseeched me to fulfill my promise. I finally gave in.

Thomas Doyle Hall, Jr., without fail, in 54 years of writing to one another, never ceased to ask, "Are you writing?" I knew he believed in me.

Lois Ames, my psychotherapist, the woman who set me free and changed my life. She is the one who pointed me to Radcliffe and Smith, a life of the intellect that I had hungered for my entire life. They engaged all my faculties and she has my gratitude—forever.

Nancy Penhume, my financial advisor, who had known me for 20 minutes when she wrote out a personal check for my tuition to the Radcliffe Seminars Program and told me "Yes, go to Smith."

Dr. Faye Crosby, psychology professor and advisor for my Smith Scholar project. Without her tireless efforts on my behalf and her belief in my work I would have never completed the manuscript. She stood in the gap for me, and as Lyndon Johnson would say, "She is someone to take to the well." (Look it up.)

Dr. Bonnie Strickland, whom I met near the end of my senior year at Smith. She invited me to be guest speaker for her Psychology of Women course. Although I had never read any of my work to anyone, I accepted, once she assured me that none of my language would get her into trouble. Ten years later, Professor Strickland informed me that students were still calling her to find out where they could get my book.

Jim Glickman, my Radcliffe Seminars professor, who encouraged me to not be afraid to offer witness to my life. He reassured me on the first day of class that I was not fundamentally writing about sex, but that I was writing about giving, and loss, and sex, and death, and self-abnegation, and self-oblivion.

Dr. Lucy Daniels, who saw me twice, for free, to help me understand why I could not publish. And sent me an angel in the form of an editor.

Dawn Shamp, my editor, who never once tried to change the way I write. She never once was horrified by my directness or sexuality. Her ethics and integrity—immediately—captured my heart. Her kindness nurtured my efforts. I could not have read the chapter on Robert one more time without her loving arm, figuratively, around my shoulder and my heart. Her gentle nature sustained me. She was quite literally an answered prayer.

Dr. Gregory Dray, who my internist sent me to for medication for depression, not only helped with that problem but championed my writing and encouraged me every step of the way. I never thought I would consult a male or a psychiatrist, but he has been my closest ally throughout this process with love (not physical) patience and attention. "Been witness to" is the phrase that comes to mind. I know he is on my side and wants good things for me.

Desire Makes the Difference

Donna Janis, my oldest girlfriend (although 16 years younger than I) who lived this story with me, has read every draft of everything I have ever written and she did most of the punctuation corrections using Track Changes.

Should this book have any success, there are at least five other books in my files. I will be dead, but Donna will know the details and has the gift to organize. Dawn has the gift to write and edit without changing the author's intent. Christopher can cover the technical factors. Ted, as my power of attorney, can manage the finances. Tim will be my agent.

Everyone in this story, with the exception of Michael and Dick, is still alive. So any future writing will be my writing.

No one named means that individual espouses my lifestyle lived during these years.